Gracie Gone

CAROL SOLOWAY

Printed and bound in the United States of America
ISBN: 978-0-578-42037-0

CHAPTER I

A lexandra Rose ran her fingers along the rim of the cold porcelain bathtub, the very bathtub where Harper had died, right here, in this house, Harper's house. Yes, even now, two years after Harper's death, this was still Harper's house, a house where the dead woman's presence was felt, sometimes even more than that of the living.

Featured in *Architectural Digest*, this house was perfect, almost too perfect. The white walls with the black crown molding throughout were striking, dramatic, the optimum backdrop for every piece of ultramodern furniture. The couches and chairs, tastefully upholstered in black and white with bursts of red, were precisely arranged. The original works of art throughout the house whispered *expensive*. Everything Harper had touched was elegant, tasteful, perfect.

Wondering whether she'd ever learn the details of how Harper died, Alex turned away from the bathtub and went to the bedroom, the bedroom she shared with Harper's widowed husband. Through a newlywed's prism of love, she looked at her husband, David, sleeping peacefully. She bent down and touched his hair ever so gently.

David was a good man, open and giving, except for the part of him he kept secret, guarded, cordoned off from everyone, including her—the part of him that still belonged to Harper. And whenever Harper's name was mentioned, he became uncomfortable, agitated. He'd even turn away ever so slightly, unable to resume the conversation, his focus lost. In time, Alex reassured herself, as their bond strengthened, Harper's pull on him would lessen.

Alex left their bedroom and walked down the hall to check on the children. Just as she started to close her youngest son's bedroom door, he called to her.

"Mommy, don't shut my door 'cause Honey won't be able to open it if she comes to sleep with me tonight."

She went to her seven-year-old son's bedside and kissed him. "Cookie Face, I told you Honey is so happy in heaven playing with the other dogs, she might not want to leave heaven."

"Mommy, I miss my Honey."

"Jon, Honey still loves you." Alex hugged him. Her heart melted, knowing how much he loved Honey, their beloved dog who'd run into the street and been killed by a reckless teenage driver. Even though they'd recently rescued Lucky, a fabulous black Labrador Retriever, Jon still wanted his Honey.

Alex rubbed noses with him, their little ritual. Wishing she could take away his pain, but Alex knew when you lose the one you love, nothing can replace the loss, the pain. She pulled Jon's cover up and kissed him.

"Love you," she said, almost calling him "baby," but she caught herself. Here in this house, it was established that Gracie, David's daughter, was the only baby. Jon insisted he was no longer the youngest and, therefore, had more privileges such as staying up half an hour later. Alex had agreed, eager for her boys to adjust to living with the new family they'd created just three months ago when she and David married.

"Maybe Honey doesn't know how to find my new room." Jon looked at her quizzically. He was thrilled with his room—formerly Harper's office. The sophisticated office, once a hub for the charity benefits and other functions Harper had coordinated, now had Jon's car bed, car wallpaper, and a highly polished tongue-in-groove wood floor that accommodated all his train tracks. Stripping the room of Harper's perfectly coordinated furniture and dramatic ultramodern pieces of art had been almost like defacing a beautiful edifice.

"Cookie Face, go to sleep." Alex left his room and went down the hall to check on Daniel.

"Mom, why are you walking around again?" Daniel, her thirteen-year-old son, asked. Always concerned about everyone, especially his mother, he'd been so helpful and accommodating during the move to Harper's house.

When David had offered to convert his study into a bedroom for Daniel, he was thrilled. Daniel, the consummate reader, insisted the book-lined shelves throughout the room were perfect for him. He'd begged David to leave his medical journals, textbooks, and classics. He even opted for a single bed pushed against the wall in order to accommodate the huge desk. More like a study than a bedroom, this was Daniel's dream room.

"I asked why you're up," Daniel repeated.

"I was just checking on Jon," she said, and walked into Daniel's room. She picked up the book that was on his night table: *The Fountainhead.* "I loved this book. We'll have to talk about it tomorrow."

"Individualism versus conformity," Daniel said. "I'm ready."

She nodded and laid the book on the nightstand, knowing it would lead to another of their deep and intellectual conversations—so unlike her First Friday Book Club, where whenever one of the women had a relationship issue, it took precedence over discussing the monthly novel selection.

"Love you." She kissed his cheek, appreciative of him and how their conversations, always charged and interesting, fed her soul.

She walked out of his room and went down the hallway. Passing the Do Not Disturb sign on the doorknob to Eric's room, she smiled. Her fifteen-year-old son, who'd been given the first choice of bedrooms when they'd moved in, had selected the guest room with the queen-sized bed and the private bath. This room exceeded even his expectations. For years, he'd begged Alex for his own room, but the house in Brea wasn't big enough. Reluctantly, he'd shared a room with Daniel. But this huge house, designed for Harper, David, and Gracie, easily accommodated Alex and her three sons.

Then she tiptoed past Gracie's room, careful not to wake David's six-year-old daughter, who rarely slept through the night.

"Daddy," Gracie called.

Alex knew it was futile to go to Gracie; she only wanted her daddy. And her cries would often escalate until her father came to her room to comfort her.

"Daddy. Daddy." Gracie's voice grew louder. "I need you now."

David bolted past Alex.

"Gracie girl, what is it?" David asked his daughter.

"Daddy, I saw her."

"Who?" he asked.

"Mommy," Gracie said. "She was walking past my room."

"Gracie girl, you were having a dream." David sat down on the bed and held her. "Mommy's in heaven."

"No," Gracie said. "I'm sure I saw her." The child pointed to the hallway where Alex stood.

"It was me," Alex said, wanting to hug Gracie, to show her love, but she knew it would take time for Gracie to accept her.

Gracie sobbed into the belly of her Chicken Love, her favorite stuffed animal, the one with the bright yellow chicken and the baby chick attached to it. "I wanted it to be my mommy, not her."

Alex knew how difficult the past two years since Gracie's mother died had to have been for her. During the day, she was often a happy, giggly six-year-old, especially when she was with her daddy and her grandma Cecile, but nights were different. According to David, Gracie's nightmares had escalated the past three months, right after he and Alex married, right after Alex and her three sons moved in.

Gracie pointed to Alex and angrily exclaimed, "You tried to trick me."

"Sweetie," Alex whispered, "I wasn't trying to fool you." Actually, from the pictures Alex had seen of Harper, it was obvious they did share a strong physical resemblance. At first, when Alex had looked at the albums, she was shocked by the similarities. They both had long brown hair, hazel eyes, and were slim. Even their taste in clothes, sporty but tailored, was exactly the same. Sometimes, she wondered whether that was why David had been attracted to her.

Alex moved closer to Gracie's bed and leaned against the post of the huge pink, lavender, and white striped canopy. This frilly, girly room was the only room that wasn't stark, contemporary, and brushed in red, black, and white. She reached over to touch the six-year-old's shoulder. "Sweetie, sometimes when a mommy—"

"You don't know about my mommy." Gracie pulled away.

"My mommy died too," Alex said.

"Were you little like me?"

"No, but big people can miss their mother and . . ."

"Really?" Gracie looked up at Alex.

As Alex sat down on the bed and tried to put her arm around Gracie, she smelled something sweet and fruity. "Gracie, are you wearing perfume?"

David looked at Gracie but said nothing. Alex was sure he noticed it. He had to have.

"Grandma gave it to me, and she said I could wear it whenever I get lonely."

"That was so lovely of your grandma Cecile to have given it to you," Alex said. She knew how wonderful Cecile had been in helping Gracie cope with Harper's death. But Cecile, too, was distraught; she faced the death of her only daughter, a loss so horrific it was visceral.

Gracie picked up her Chicken Love. "Grandma said it would be like Mommy's always around me."

"Yes," Alex said. She knew for a little girl, there was nothing like a mother's love. She rubbed the scar on her right wrist, the scar from the time her mother's cigarette supposedly fell and landed on Alex's wrist. Yes, it was an accident, or at least that's what her mother had said and what everyone believed. Even as Alex had watched her mother deliberately snub out the cigarette onto her wrist, she needed to believe it was an accident.

Alex knew about the void a daughter felt without a mother's love. She reached out to Gracie. "I know how much you miss your mommy."

"You don't know how much my mommy loved me," Gracie sobbed while David stroked her long brown hair and held her and Chicken Love in his arms.

"All mommies love their little girls," Alex said, and knew that was what little girls had to think, even when reality proved

6

otherwise. Because if they couldn't trust their mother's love, then the world couldn't ever be safe.

"Why were you coming into my room?" Gracie asked, obviously embarrassed about being caught wearing perfume—that perfume.

"Sweetie, I was just checking on the boys," Alex said.

Gracie pouted and put her arms around her father's neck. "Daddy, why'd you forget to tuck me in tonight?"

"Alex, why were you walking around again?" David whispered.

"I couldn't sleep." She knew David had no idea how often she'd get up, walk past each room, and wonder what Harper and David had done there. Had they laughed there? Had they made love there? But she also knew how much David loved her and how effortlessly he'd embraced her boys. She decided she couldn't allow her insecurity about a dead woman's memory to overshadow and tarnish the present. But sometimes it did.

"Please." David leaned over and kissed Alex's forehead. "Go back to bed. I'll be there soon."

"No, Daddy, I need you to stay with me like Mommy always did whenever I got scared."

"Gracie, what scares you?" Alex asked.

Gracie turned away. "I don't want to talk. Talking doesn't make the bad things go away."

"What bad things?" Alex asked. She wished she could fill at least some of the void in Gracie's heart while still preserving Harper's memory. That's what she longed for and hoped to create and nurture in their new family.

"I'm fine with handling this," David said, an uncharacteristic edge to his voice. Then he turned to Gracie and softly promised, "I'll make sure there are no bad things to scare you. I'm here to protect you. Always."

CHAPTER 2

David returned to bed and wrapped his arms around Alex. "Gracie told me she was sorry she was rude to you."

"I understand," Alex said. "Losing her mother when she was only four is horrific. I'm sure the perfume helps her—something of Harper's to hold on to when she feels scared or lonely."

Alex knew Cecile, Harper's mother, had been Gracie's primary caregiver from the time Harper had died, actually from when she became ill until Alex had moved into the house. But the way Cecile ambled about the house with a familiarity Alex hadn't yet embraced was a constant reminder the house was still Harper's.

David drew his wife to him. "When you're home more . . ."

"Soon," she said. She'd thought about selling her chiropractic practice in order to attend her children's games and other activities. She'd been working long hours, first because she loved it and second because she'd borrowed so much money to pay the attorneys while fighting for her children in the child-custody battle with her former husband, Gabe.

"Alex, you know you don't have to work."

"I know, and I do want to spend more time with the children while they're still young, but I also enjoy working." Yes, she knew all too well how transitory childhood was. It had been devastating for her and the boys during those several months when she'd lost custody. Her former husband had twisted the details of the time she accidentally burned Jon, their then-four-year-old son, and had colluded with the forensic psychiatrist, his personal friend, to try to establish she was a danger to the children.

After their protracted court battle, she'd prevailed and regained custody. Now, she was determined, no one would ever question her competency as a mother, and she was going to be a wonderful stepmom to Gracie—that she vowed to herself and owed to David.

Appreciative of her new life and the promise of serenity and stability, she smiled at David.

He held her close.

She knew he wanted to make life easier for her, but he also wanted to provide a stable family for Gracie. Harper had been able to build her wildly successful and highly sought-after interior design business around Gracie's schedule, but as a chiropractor, there was no way Alex could do that—especially now that she'd moved so far away from her practice.

And although Alex was a dedicated and successful chiropractor, she was willing to give it all up for her family. After she'd lost custody of her children and gone through the horrific and poisonous court battle, Alex had come to a new appreciation of how precious time with her children was. Just last week, Jon had cried because she couldn't leave work to attend his school play. He'd claimed all the other mothers were there except his. Disappointing him broke her heart. The myth about having it all wasn't working for her, at least not while the children were young.

David twirled her hair around his finger and nodded. "Alex, you know I'm going to support you in whatever decision you make."

"I was thinking we should probably hire someone to help Cecile," Alex said. "Sometimes she seems overwhelmed with all the activities."

"It would be too disruptive for Gracie. I don't want her to have yet another change, and she loves Cecile."

Alex also knew there was no arguing with David about Gracie; he was adamant about protecting her, making sure her childhood was void of any more pain and loss. And Alex also wanted to care for Gracie, but that would come in time.

"It's late," Alex said, too tired to start a conversation about how resentful Gracie sometimes was about the fact that Alex and her boys had moved into "her" house.

"I'm sorry if anything she said hurt you." He kissed her. "Love you."

"You too." She did love him, absolutely adored him and was so grateful he'd entered her life. But she wondered whether she really knew him. Sure, she knew how he curled into his pillow and how he sometimes called out in his sleep. Yes, she was the only one in the world who knew intimate details about David, but did she really know him? There was a secret he had, of that she was certain, but he kept it hidden, guarded.

She thought it truly wasn't possible to ever know another. She'd learned that from her former husband, the man she'd thought was an honest, loving husband and a compassionate physician, only to find he was neither. Therefore, whenever anything was amiss, Alex would become cautious, hopeful she wouldn't find anything to confirm her fear that maybe, just maybe, David knew more about Harper's death than he shared.

There'd been nothing to confirm her fears, and for that she was thankful. Still, she knew horrific things could happen on the other side of marriage—the side where dreams imploded, and people weren't who they seemed.

◆ ◆ ◆

"Daddy." Gracie ran to David's side of the bed. She pressed her nose against his cheek.

He opened his eyes and looked at the clock. "Gracie girl, it's too early."

"Please." Gracie started to crawl into bed next to David. He moved closer to Alex, turned toward Gracie, and tickled her belly.

Gracie giggled. Then she put her head on her father's chest and fell asleep.

David gently scooped her up and took her back to her room.

When he returned to bed, he kissed Alex. "I love you and so does Gracie. She'll stay in her room in time. Are you okay with it?"

He always asked Alex how she was doing following Gracie's unexpected visits to their bedroom. Alex knew it would take time for their families to blend together. There were so many details to work out, but Alex was sure they would. Her boys genuinely liked Gracie, maybe almost loved her. And Gracie adored the boys, referring to the older ones as her "biggest brothers," and she and Jon had become fast friends from the moment they met. They were always plotting something, sharing some secret, bursting to reveal it to anyone who pressed or offered some reward—that was, when they weren't teasing one another.

But it wasn't only Gracie who had to adjust to the loss of a parent. The boys were trying to cope with their father's impending sentencing for Medicare fraud and another trial regarding his charges for solicitation of murder for hire and conspiracy to commit murder—Alex's murder. Yes, her former husband had resorted to attempted murder when it looked like he wasn't going to be granted sole custody of the children as he'd planned. He'd actually hired someone to thwart Alex from gaining custody of her children—forever.

The boys had been embarrassed by the rumors in the community about their father's actions, and that was the main reason they were relieved about moving to David's house in Laguna Beach and changing schools. But Gabe was still their dad, and they were permitted to and did visit him. On the day before their scheduled meeting with him, they were quiet. Then, when they'd return home, they were often completely silent for hours, sometimes days.

Alex knew, in part, the boys blamed her for what had happened to their dad. They couldn't accept the truth of their father's deception and diabolical plan to destroy her. Children always turned a blind eye to their parents' flaws; they had to or else they'd have no one else to believe in, to trust. She'd done the same with her mother; she knew it all too well.

"You okay?" David repeated.

"We're all doing great. Don't worry." Alex kissed his neck and then got out of bed. She went to the bathroom. After applying her makeup, she came out of the bathroom and started to put on her crisp white blouse and navy skirt.

"Come here, beautiful." He beckoned her to him.

"There are four very hungry children downstairs." She laughed.

Bare-chested, sprawled across the bed, he was muscled, toned. At forty-eight, he had the body of an athlete.

"Mmm," she murmured and walked to the bed.

He reached for her and pulled her to him. "Love you."

"Love you more," she said. Yes, she was living the life she'd never even dared to dream of three years ago when her former husband left her.

12

"Alex, let me hold you for just a few minutes."

"Right." She laughed and tousled his hair. "Gotta go down and make breakfast for the kids."

"I've got a better idea." He winked. "Cold cereal for them and hot sex for us."

Drawn to him, she decided tomorrow would be a perfect day for French toast and started to unbutton her blouse.

"Mommy, get me out of here," Jon screamed from downstairs.

She looked at David apologetically. "Make it up to you tonight."

CHAPTER 3

She ran downstairs and saw Jon, wearing his pajamas, locked in the dog cage with Lucky. "What happened?" she asked, wondering why Lucky was in the cage, which they rarely used.

"Mommy, get the latch open," Jon yelled.

Gracie was standing next to the cage and giggling.

Jon crinkled his nose. "I wanted to see what it was like to be in a jail. So, I got Lucky's cage, and we both got in. But then Gracie came and turned the latch. It's scary like jail where my daddy's going."

Alex was worried about Jon's fears, but she thought Gracie was just being a little mischievous, having some fun. Alex looked at her sternly but said nothing. It was the rule—each parent would discipline their own child; therefore, she was reluctant to chastise the girl. The rule worked most of the time, and Alex knew her boys weren't ready for David to step into the role of father—not yet.

"I don't like it in jail, and my daddy won't either." Jon started to cry. "Why's my daddy going to jail anyway?"

"We'll talk about it tonight. Right now, you have to get ready for school."

She went to unlock the latch.

"Tell me now," Jon insisted.

"Later," she said. She didn't want Gracie to hear too much. She wouldn't understand, and talk about jail could frighten her. Alex also wondered exactly what her former husband had told the boys about his possible imprisonment for Medicare fraud.

"Thanks for rescuing me," Jon said with a whistle, typical of the front-tooth-missing seven-year-old he was.

"Cookie Face," Alex said, using Jon's pet name, the name she'd use whenever he'd scrunch up his nose and look at her with his big brown eyes. Wondering if it were possible for her to love him even more, she promised, "I'll always take care of my baby."

"I'm not a baby, but you can take care of me until I'm big," Jon said.

Alex kissed him, confident, now that she'd regained custody, this was a promise she would keep to him as well as to her other two boys.

Jon scampered away from the cage, yanking Gracie's long brown hair as he walked past her.

"Ouch," Gracie yelled.

David called from upstairs. "Is everything okay down there?"

"Everything's fine." Alex put her finger to her lips and winked at the little girl.

Gracie gave her a high five and wrapped her spindly arms around Alex's legs—the first time she'd ever showed affection without David's prompting.

"Mommy, why are you being on her side?" Jon tried to push Gracie away from his mother. "Gracie was mean to me."

"I'm not mean." Tears welled in Gracie's big blue eyes.

"Gracie girl," David called as he came downstairs. "Did you do something that I have to call Santa and tell him to take back your

American Girl doll?" he asked. He never raised his voice to Gracie. He'd calmly explain what she did to displease him and how important it was to behave. Then he'd give her a punishment—usually the loss of a privilege such as watching a television program.

"Jon, go upstairs and put on your clothes," Alex said. "And you are never to pull her hair again."

"She started it." Jon stuck out his tongue at Gracie.

"Jon. Upstairs." Alex turned and walked into the kitchen to make breakfast. The stark white kitchen with the steel appliances, all top of the line, gleaming, and massive, exactly what she would have picked if she had the unlimited funds that it had to have taken. And the kitchen table, commissioned from an artist who made signature tabletops, black and white with a touch of red swirled in a dramatic pattern, perfectly complemented this amazing kitchen.

Gracie pulled on David's pant leg. "Daddy, Jon hurt my hair."

"I think something else happened before that." David picked up his daughter and looked at her eye to eye. "Do you want to tell me what happened?"

"No, thank you, but thanks for asking," Gracie said as her father put her down.

Alex and David shared a wink, stifling a laugh. Sometimes it was hard to be stern, especially when the children gave a funny retort. Simple rituals brought Alex the most joy, and a family breakfast was no exception. She felt a satisfaction that she'd thought she'd never recapture. And the best part was that the "dad chair" was no longer empty, providing the most wonderful symmetry to the family and her life.

Eric threw his backpack on the vestibule floor and kicked it to the corner. He turned his baseball cap backwards, typical of the fifteen-year-old jock he was, and took his seat at the table.

"Eric, cap off," Alex said.

"At my dad's—"

"Here we don't wear baseball caps at the table." She didn't want to hear what he was able to do at his dad's. Whenever he'd cite the privileges he was given at his father's house, or anything about his father for that matter, her chest would tighten. Eric reminded her of Gabe; he even talked like his father. Even the inflection of his voice was Gabe, pure Gabe.

"Where's Daniel?" David asked, obviously annoyed that he was late once again.

Since all four children went to different schools, every morning Alex and David drove to two schools each. David drove Gracie to a private kindergarten which was right near Daniel's middle school. Alex drove Jon to the elementary school and Eric to high school.

"Daniel, get down here at once," Alex called up.

"You need to talk to him," David said, pouring himself a cup of coffee and making a cup of tea for his wife.

"Daddy, this weekend, can we watch *Frozen?*" Gracie asked, her conversation directed at David, clearly excluding everyone else at the kitchen table.

Eric piled the French toast onto his plate. "*Frozen's* the worst."

"Eric," Alex said as she cut Jon's French toast. "Leave some for Daniel."

"I gotta bulk up, Mom. Danny's too busy being a nerd to care about important things like sports," Eric said.

"Protein improves muscle tone." Alex got up and grabbed the protein powder. "I'm making you a shake."

"Me too," Jon said, holding up his empty glass and almost knocking over his mother's cup of tea.

"Doofus, be careful," Eric said. "I'm not going through another burn."

"An accident, you mean," Alex said, referring to the time she'd burned Jon's leg, the time everything got turned inside out, the time Jon's burned leg caused her to lose custody of the children.

Daniel ran into the kitchen and patted Gracie's head as he took his seat.

Gracie smiled up at him. "Danny, you want to see *Frozen* with me. Right?"

Daniel took one piece of French toast and nodded at her. "*Frozen's* fine with me."

Eric scowled at him. "I'm going to my dad's house on Sunday. I don't want to see any of the little kids' stupid movies."

Alex started to clear the table. "Daniel, where's your science project?"

David winked at Daniel, who was just wolfing down his last bite. "We put his project in the car last night. Everything's under control."

"I guess you guys don't need me." She smiled.

David scooped up his daughter, kissed Alex, and left with Daniel following close behind. Their routes, as well as all of their routines, were carefully coordinated around their children's schedules as well as their work: carpooling, meal preparation, putting the younger children to bed—everything.

As she was cleaning up from breakfast, Alex placed the syrup back in the pantry. She saw a bag seemingly hidden on the upper shelf. It hadn't been there before, or if it had, she hadn't noticed it. It crinkled as she unfolded the top. She looked in the bag, saw syringes, and panicked.

"Mom, come on or I'll be late," Eric called to her.

She rushed to the car, buckled Jon into his car seat, and hesitated. Tonight, she would ask David why he'd brought the syringes home and why he'd hidden them. She reassured herself—there was a simple explanation. There had to be.

CHAPTER 4

Alex slammed on the brakes, avoiding the Jeep that passed the stop sign and almost sideswiped their car. Her chest tightened, and she reminded herself she had to concentrate on the road. There was probably a perfectly good reason for the bag of syringes she'd found in the pantry.

"Mom, are you looking where you're going?" Eric scowled.

"Of course I am," she said.

"Mommy!" Jon called from the back seat. "Are you going right?"

"Jon, we'll be at your school in a few minutes," she said. "And Eric, see how you have to watch all sides?"

"I have six months before I take driver's ed."

"It'll be here before you know it." Alex reached across and patted Eric's arm. Amazing how quickly time had passed. He was shaving, voice deepening, and soon he'd be driving. Now that the boys were living with her again, she savored the time she had with them.

"My lunch," Eric yelled. "We have to go back."

"We can't," she said. "I've got too many patients waiting."

"Dad would turn around and go home." He shook his head.

She was already running late for the office. The commute was becoming untenable and being away from the children for that long each day, especially Jon, was wearing on her—and them. And David had offered, he'd even insisted, he was willing and definitely able to pay for everything. In addition to her legal costs, he'd offered to pay for her children's college when the time came. Since her former husband was enmeshed in his legal nightmare, he'd never be able to pay anything toward the boys' college tuition. There were days when she almost accepted David's offer to "just quit the practice."

"Hello," Eric called. "Are we going back or not?"

"Mommy," Jon cried out from the back seat. "I don't want to go home. I need to give the teacher my homework."

Eric scowled. "What lame first-grade homework could be so important?"

"Every grade matters, especially the first one." Alex quickly turned back to give Jon a thumbs-up. "Eric, take money out of my purse for lunch."

Eric folded his arms across his chest. "School lunches are disgusting. Dad would go back," he repeated.

Deciding to put an end to Eric's incessant references to his father's parenting, she reminded him, "It doesn't matter what your father would do. You're not living with your dad, and—"

"Yeah," Eric said. "Dad told me about—"

"Whatever he said about me wasn't true." She knew whatever Gabe said was colored by his desire to discredit and destroy her. She knew Eric emailed his dad every day; she couldn't stop that, but she was going to make him understand the truth, not his father's prismatic version of it.

"Dad said he never did any of the things you accused him of. Dad said you just made problems so David and you could be a family."

"I didn't even know David when your father—"

"Dad told me he didn't do anything wrong."

"Eric, your father wanted to have me killed," she yelled. But as horrific as her former husband had been to her, she knew how difficult it was for Eric to accept.

"I'm sure Dad wouldn't have had you killed," Eric said.

"Mommy, you can't die," Jon said. "Gracie told me when the mommy dies, it's bad. Really, really bad."

"Why did you make them arrest my father?" Eric scowled.

"Mommy, I asked if you're going to die."

"Eric, I didn't make them arrest him, and Jon, I'm not dying." She was amazed at how totally different the two versions were: Jon feared the loss of his mother just like Gracie, and Eric blamed her for the loss of his father.

"Boys, we're a family, and—"

Eric shook his head. "No, my family isn't David and Gracie."

"Let me finish."

Jon kicked the back of Eric's seat. "It's not polite to interrupt big people."

Eric turned back and looked at Jon. "Doofus, it's rude to kick."

Another driver honked at her. She'd almost cut him off.

"Don't get in an accident about it," Eric said.

"I'm watching," she said. She was trying to remain calm. Eric had been the one who'd really wanted to live with his father after the divorce. And he'd been resolute during the custody case, shutting her out whenever she'd tried to get close to him.

But she was no longer going to allow his version of Gabe as the good father to cloud the truth. She'd been blind to Gabe's addiction to cocaine, blind to his fraudulent Medicare billing. Yes, she'd been blind to everything, especially to his hiring Luke to discredit her and then, when that didn't work and it looked like she'd regain custody of the children, to murder her. Even

21

then, she'd refused to believe it. She couldn't fathom Gabe being that evil—that was, until he was.

"Mom, Jon's school," Eric yelled.

"Mommy," Jon said, "you didn't answer me. When are you going to die?"

"I told you, I'm not going to die for a long time." She leaned back and patted Jon's leg.

Jon pulled his leg away. "Mommy, that was my bad leg."

She quickly glanced back at him. "I remember, but the burn was a long time ago, and you don't have any scars."

She pulled into the drop-off line.

When they came to a stop, Eric turned back to Jon. "Get out quickly."

Jon unbuckled his car seat belt. "My leg is still bad. That's what my daddy said." Jon collected his backpack, kissed Alex goodbye, and sauntered off.

As he shut the car door, she called after him, "Love you."

Once Jon left, her conversations with Eric during the short drive from Jon's school to his high school were usually directed at coordinating rides for after-school practice and reminding Eric to be polite to Gracie's grandmother when she took care of them in the afternoons. Today, she needed to have a real conversation with him. "I told you the truth. Your dad wanted Luke to harm me."

"I thought Luke was your 'boyfriend.'"

"Please, I know this is hard for you."

"You don't know. They're going to put my dad in prison." He turned away. "Just because you wanted to marry David."

She was determined to tell him the truth but also wanted to be cautious about upsetting him. It was difficult to delicately explain how Gabe, his father, had hired Luke to derail her from the custody hearings, and then when it looked as though the judge wasn't going to award him sole custody, Gabe's demands had escalated.

Gabe and Luke had met during a plumbing job at Gabe's house. Luke told her when he'd gone to Gabe's garage to check the water heater, he saw tennis racquets and initiated a conversation about tennis. They'd talked for a while, a long while. Then Gabe, who assumed he could buy anyone—that had always worked for him—had offered Luke money and membership to the Brea Tennis Club, where Alex was still a member. All Luke had to do was take Alex out and distract her during the custody case. The deal seemed easy, or so Luke had thought.

When things turned, and the custody battle wasn't going as Gabe had planned, he'd not only needed Luke to tarnish Alex's credibility by taking her out until all hours of the night and making sure she missed appointments with the forensic psychiatrist, he'd needed Luke to make her disappear—completely.

When Luke had refused, Gabe threatened to report him for allegedly stealing his fiancée's diamond ring and raping her. Gabe had probably assumed, as a prominent physician, his allegations would be credible, and Luke, a lowly plumber whose company happened to have sent him out to Gabe's house on a plumbing emergency, would never be able to refute his claim. Luke knew the consequences of coming forward with that information, but at the final custody hearing, he'd revealed Gabe's plan and his involvement in it. He'd even recorded Gabe's conversations on his cell phone.

"Mom, this is all just because you wanted to marry David," Eric repeated, pulling her back to their conversation.

"Eric, you and I were getting along so well, until—"

"Until my dad told me the truth."

"It's not the truth. The truth is your dad and I were in love, we married and had you guys, and then your dad—"

"Dad told me not to listen to you if you try to explain stuff."

"You have to hear this whether you want to or not because it's the truth."

He folded his hands across his chest, defiant. "Your truth."

"Maybe, but at least hear me." She was sweating; she had to make him understand who his father was and what he'd done.

He rolled his eyes and looked at her, challenging her. "Go."

"Your dad fell in love with Linda and didn't want me. But then he and Linda decided they wanted you boys to live with them, and—"

"We were all happy living at Linda's house before you messed it up."

"Then your father and I got into the terrible custody battle."

"Mom, why couldn't you just let us go?"

"What are you even thinking?" she yelled. Then she caught herself. She needed to explain how a mother couldn't just let her children go, but she knew if she got too emotional, then he'd clam up. "Listen, your dad and Linda, maybe they were doing drugs, but—"

"Stop," he demanded.

"No," she said. "They decided to hire Luke. I didn't know they paid him to join the tennis club and everything—to take me out."

"Why'd he take money to date you? What kind of a creep would do that?"

She knew it was easy for him to see Luke as evil; he'd never liked Luke and had made it known. "Luke had terrible debt after his daughter died. He was going to lose his house, and his children would have had to drop out of college."

"I don't care about Luke," he shouted.

"You're right," she agreed. "But you have to know your dad wanted Luke to kill me."

"Dad would never do that. He told me you made everything up because you were angry that we wanted to live with him. He said you could do things to us, like the time you burned Jon's leg."

Her gut twisted. She needed him to understand. "You know it was an accident. You were there." Then she realized sometimes even when people saw things, their mind could twist it; reality was distorted by what they believed, not just what they saw. Her son wanted to believe she was the evil one, and that crushed her.

"Mom, as hard as I try, I can't remember how the teakettle fell onto Jon's legs. Sometimes I'm sure Jon knocked it out of your hand, and other times I think you just dropped it. It's so confusing. Why do you and my dad hate each other?"

"Your dad was addicted to drugs, and that can make a person say things, do things—"

"No, my dad's a doctor."

She knew how much he revered his father. Unconditional love wasn't just felt by a parent for a child. As a matter of fact, a child's love for his parent was the truest form of unconditional love. The parent, however evil, is all the child knows. The way each parent treats their child is the child's only experience of love—that she knew very well, too well.

She looked at him. "Please," she said softly, insisting he listen and hoping he'd understand a truth that was definitely more than a fifteen-year-old boy should have to face.

"Okay, Mom, tell me your story," Eric said, almost in despair.

It wasn't one of his brother Jon's soft requests for a bedtime story. It was a challenge. This was the moment her relationship with Eric was being tested. She had to prove his father was evil, evil beyond anything he could imagine. If not, she'd lose Eric forever.

"I promise I'm telling you the truth."

"Dad said the same." He turned away. "Go on."

"Luke recorded your dad and Linda. They threatened him. If he didn't 'get rid' of me, then they were going to go to the police and show he'd done terrible things like . . ." She couldn't tell him they'd threatened to reveal he'd raped Linda; no, it was better to just tell him they were going to accuse Luke of stealing Linda's diamond ring.

"Did Luke take the ring?"

"No, he wouldn't steal anything."

"But he took money from my father to go out with you. This is getting sick."

"Yes, the whole thing was a nightmare, a horrific nightmare."

Eric started to sob. "Why did this happen to our family?"

"I don't know. Sometimes we want something or someone so badly that we do things, horrible things, to get what we want."

"Mom, this is too complicated. I need time to think."

She wanted to pull over and give him a hug but knew he had to get to school. "We'll talk about it tonight. Try not to think about it now."

"Fat chance of that." He wiped his eyes.

"I love you," she said.

As he got out of the car, he turned to her and hesitantly said, "You too."

CHAPTER 5

Alex pulled into the reserved parking space at her chiropractic office a few minutes earlier than usual. She was sorry she'd refused to turn around and go home to retrieve Eric's lunch, but it was better to teach him to plan ahead. Eric—and all the other boys, for that matter—sometimes had difficulty with the fact that her chiropractic office was so far from their new home in Laguna Beach. When they'd lived five minutes from her office, she was able to adjust her schedule and leave for fifteen to twenty minutes in order to transport the boys to their activities.

And now that Seth, her former business partner, had moved to Arizona, there was no one to cover the practice when she needed to leave to attend her children's events. After seeing how upset Jon was last week when she couldn't go to his school play, she'd even considered just closing the office. Now that Gabe was consumed with his legal issues, the boys had only her to witness and share their victories. It was impossible to do it all, even though she desperately wanted to.

After treating her morning patients, Alex was determined to leave the office on time to make the February lunch meeting of her First Friday Book Club. Since they'd all been so busy during the holidays, they'd canceled both the December and the January meetings.

Alex put her copy of this month's novel, *The Husband's Secret,* into her briefcase and drove to Waters Restaurant. As soon as she arrived, she saw Liz, already seated and checking herself in her pocket mirror. Liz was a little older than the others in the First Friday Book Club, but she was stylish and always dressed in the latest fashion. And today was no exception. She wore a soft coral dress with a long, cultured pearl necklace—tasteful, classic.

Alex hugged her best friend. "Liz, I'd expect to see Meredith admiring herself in her glitzy Swarovski crystal mirror, but you?" For the past eight years, their friendship had been unwavering. Liz was the reason she was able to move on after her divorce, and for that she was grateful.

"Thought I was peeling."

Alex sat down next to Liz. "Your tan is fabulous."

"The fringe benefit of friends over forty—can't see without glasses, but I *am* peeling."

"You're almost as gorgeous as Meredith," Alex teased. No, Liz wasn't as attractive as Meredith; none of them were. Meredith was beautiful. She knew it and used it.

"Did I hear you mention *moi*?" Meredith approached, perfectly coiffed and elegant in her business suit; Chanel, of course. She gave Alex and Liz air kisses and took her seat.

Liz reached out and touched Meredith's exquisitely soft leather bag. "New purse?"

"Of course. What would Christmas be without a new Louis Vuitton? And speaking of gifts, Alex, are those new earrings I see?" Meredith nodded approvingly.

"From David," Alex said, and touched the earrings. They were beautiful, but try as hard as she could, there was the nagging fear they could have been Harper's. The tentacles of the past sometimes wrapped around her so tightly they smothered the joy of the present. "The earrings are just a little too ostentatious for work, but . . ."

"Don't refuse anything. You should get used to it, and speaking of aversion to luxury . . ." Meredith pointed toward Terrie, who was weaving among the tables.

"That's quite an outfit," Meredith said, glancing up disapprovingly at Terrie's long, flowered skirt and white peasant top.

Terrie twirled around, allowing the skirt to flare out. "Chico's," she said. "I just love all their clothes. My amazing husband bought it for me. You know I would never have splurged on this outfit myself."

"That's obvious," Meredith said. "And it kind of looks like your other stuff, and . . ."

"I love this style. Suits me so well," Terrie said, clearly unfazed by Meredith's chiding.

They all looked up as Judi approached. She was a perfect size two, without an ounce of fat, and her tailored red Ralph Lauren dress was exquisite, classic. With her long brown hair coiffed like Teri Hatcher, she looked like Hollywood, pure Hollywood, and in her own way, she was a little, just a little, threat to Meredith.

"Let's order. I have to get back to the office sometime today," Meredith said, and called the waitress.

The waitress came to their table and took their orders: Chinese chicken salad for all except for Terrie, who ordered her usual hamburger and French fries.

Terrie shrugged. "I was going to start my diet after the holidays, but . . ."

"You look fine," Liz said.

Alex smiled approvingly. "Absolutely."

Meredith tossed back her perfectly coiffed mane. "Nothing a little makeup, diet, wardrobe revision, and—"

"I'm not trying to look like you," Terrie said.

Meredith reached over and picked up Terrie's macramé purse. "I can see that."

Although they appeared to be diametric opposites in every way, they were best friends. Meredith was always trying to "update" Terrie, who looked like a woman of the sixties with her short bangs, curly hair, and pale skin that yearned for some makeup. Her outfits were always reminiscent of a style that time had left behind.

Terrie turned to Alex. "Did your boys like our gifts?"

"Thank you so much," Alex said, and then she turned to Meredith. "And thank you for all the outrageously generous gifts you and Warren sent for the boys and Gracie. I know they sent thank-you notes, but I should have called also."

Meredith pursed her lips. "Warren wasn't happy about being away from Gracie at Christmas, but we made the best of it—at a five-star hotel—if you can believe there are those in a third-world country like Mexico. I so wish David would get over his grudge." She tossed back a few strands of her long black hair. "We do enjoy our adorable Gracie."

"Yes." Alex nodded. "Gracie missed her uncle Warren terribly."

Obviously trying to defuse the tension, Liz held up her copy of *The Husband's Secret.* "Do you think you can ever really know another person?"

Meredith looked surprised. "Since when did we get to the book before juicy stuff?"

"Now that we're married, is there juicy stuff?" Alex asked, and then was sorry she'd said it.

"Juicy stuff." Meredith held out her arm, showing off her new emerald and diamond bracelet.

Judi tapped her million-dollar-red nails on her water glass. "What'd you do for that?"

Liz leaned over and took Meredith's wrist in her hand and nodded approvingly. Then with her usual acerbic wit, she said, "Yes, tell us exactly what you did."

"Just being *moi*." Meredith smiled. "But as far as the juicy stuff, Alex is *the* newlywed among us."

Alex's face flushed. "We have four children from six to fifteen. Between waiting up for Eric to come home and Gracie coming into our bedroom—oh, and a dog—sleep is what we crave."

"Do I detect trouble in paradise?" Meredith asked.

"Oh, no," Alex shook her head. "David is fabulous, but . . ."

Terrie tugged at her white peasant blouse. She prodded, "But?"

"But," Liz said and looked around the table. "We all probably have a little something we wish were different, something . . ."

Alex smiled at her best friend. Before moving to Laguna Beach, she and Liz would go on walks together once or twice a week. Liz would arrive at her house, ready for a walk and talk right after Alex had put Jon to sleep and finished helping the older boys with their homework. That stopped once Alex moved, as did their daily phone calls. It seemed every time Alex started to call Liz, there was something else she had to tend to.

Sorry she'd made the comment about the children being around in front of Meredith, Alex started to explain, "David's so involved in his gynecology practice, and he's still so committed to his work with the Flying Samaritans."

"It's awesome that he's so charitable, so giving," Terrie said with sincerity. She was the flower child, someone who always

31

saw the good in people. That was why her psychology practice flourished; her empathy was unparalleled.

"Yes," Alex agreed. She didn't want to complain about David, but these women were her best friends, her entire support system; well, maybe not Meredith, who'd become caustic toward her ever since Alex and David had gotten married. And, in a way, Alex did understand Warren's anger about David limiting his access to Gracie, his only niece.

The waitress delivered their Chinese chicken salads and a hamburger for Terrie.

Meredith waited and then leaned forward and lowered her head as though she was going to impart something of great importance. "You know, *The Husband's Secret* got me to wondering about... Well, Warren told me David was so involved with his work, he wasn't such a great husband to Harper or father to Gracie."

"And look at how devoted he is to Gracie now," Terrie said.

Alex nodded at Terrie. "And he works all day and then goes back in the evening. Sometimes he stays in the hospital all night, especially if one of his patients is in labor. I really worry about him."

"I'd worry more about his wife dying in a bathtub than him working so much," Judi said.

Alex knew they weren't satisfied with the details of Harper's death as presented. They'd insisted there was more, much more, to that story, except, of course, Meredith, whose husband, Harper's brother, allegedly knew exactly what happened. Yes, Alex knew about secrets—secrets people kept, secrets that would cause too much pain if shared.

"As we all know, David had been out of town when Harper died." Meredith struck a dramatic pose and said, "It was Warren, Harper's dear brother, who was with her shortly before she . . ."

Meredith's words now floated through a prism, Alex's prism of Warren's possible deception. Alex wondered if Meredith knew anything that she wasn't sharing. The First Friday Book Club had a pact: No secrets from each other, and the secrets they shared were sacred.

Meredith took a bite of salad and looked across at Alex. "I wonder what David actually says about the whole thing?"

"David says the past is too painful, and we need to keep that door locked for Gracie's sake."

"Umm." Meredith flipped back a few strands of hair. "I've been thinking, and I should really drop out of the book club. I mean, I'm too busy with work and—"

"No. I'll drop out," Alex said.

"What's going on?" Liz looked at Meredith.

"Don't you remember how we sang 'That's What Friends Are For' at my daughter's wedding?" Judi asked.

"Friendships are so important. The bonds are often even stronger than family ties. Women need friends." Terrie tugged at her blouse. "What's the issue? I'm sure we can rectify it."

"We have to," Liz said. "This book club has been together for years."

Alex, the newest member, and Meredith looked at each other, waiting for the other to speak.

The waitress refilled their glasses.

Meredith took a sip and said, "David and Warren."

Judi pointed a red fingernail at them both. "Alex, you and I had horrific tension when our husbands were going through their dispute over the hospital administration issues, but we worked it out."

"Yeah, and my husband—former, that is—left the hospital," Alex said.

Judi moved a few morsels of chicken around her salad plate. "Was thrown out due to his Medicare fraud, you mean."

Liz, an insurance agent with a thriving business, knew everything about insurance billing, and said, "Fraud is punishable by prison and significant financial consequences."

"Yes," Alex whispered. She didn't want to think about Gabe. He'd done it to himself and tried to ruin her. She was worried about the boys, especially now with their father's impending prison sentencing. And after the fraud sentencing, he would probably have weeks or even months of trial for the charges of conspiracy to commit murder.

Terrie reached across the table and patted Alex's hand. "If you need any money or—"

"She has David, remember," Meredith said sarcastically.

"I thought we were going to try to work it out," Terrie said.

"By the way, I didn't finish *The Husband's Secret*—what was the secret?" Judi asked.

"Without spoiling it, his secret—what he thought he did— never actually happened," Alex said.

"Now it's crystal clear." Judi laughed.

Liz pushed her plate away. "In the book, the husband spent his whole life punishing himself for a horrific deed that he thought he committed years ago: his former girlfriend's death. However, in actuality, she was very sick. He got angry with her, shook her, and then she died—a freak accident. The husband never knew that wasn't what caused his former girlfriend's death, and he replayed the scene over and over in his mind."

"It's like Harper's story," Meredith said.

"What is that supposed to mean?" Alex asked. In truth, there were times when she suspected it was more, much more than an accidental drowning in the bathtub.

34

Liz folded her arms across her chest, her eyeglasses clanking on her chain. "Don't torture Alex. Tell us whether David did something unethical or inappropriate."

Meredith said, "It seems David wouldn't allow Harper to try any of the alternative medical approaches Warren had researched. They argued about that, and—"

"Well, I do understand," Alex said. "I mean, even though I'm a chiropractor and some believe adjustments can help with the pain of cancer, alternative medicine is not a cure for cancer."

Wiping the ketchup from her chin, Terrie said, "Actually, the mind has miraculous power and can alter the body chemistry, but . . ."

Liz nodded. "I agree, and I understand where David, being a medical doctor, wouldn't want her to go the nonconventional route."

"There was something else," Meredith said. "Warren told me he and David got into a huge argument because Warren wanted to celebrate Harper's death with a memorial ceremony at her gravesite, and David didn't want to 'make a big fuss.'"

"I doubt David would refuse to honor Harper's memory," Alex said.

Meredith said, "You know, it was Warren who'd purchased Harper's beautiful headstone. David just wanted to scatter her ashes over the ocean and be done."

"Maybe David decided on that for Gracie's sake," Alex said. David's aversion to ceremony didn't make him an uncaring husband; it was consistent with his desire for the understated, the private. And Alex knew David had eventually capitulated to Warren and Cecile, and Harper was buried in the family plot next to her father.

Meredith flipped back several strands of her long black hair. "Warren was hurt because he thought David was being insensitive to Cecile's feelings by refusing to have a proper Catholic ceremony—which was what Harper wanted."

"David loves Harper," Alex said, and then was surprised she'd said *loves*, as though Harper were still alive. She was thinking of the nights when he'd walk through the house, and then, in the morning, she'd find the photo albums strewn across the family room floor. But she also knew he refused to talk about Harper, especially about the night she died.

"We should discuss the book," Terrie said, obviously sensing the conversation could only result in a confrontation between Meredith and Alex, each defending her husband.

Meredith put her copy of *The Husband's Secret* on the table. "Okay, speaking about the book, I've got to read something to you ladies." She opened the book and read, "Tess was busy with mundane married life."

"Okay, what's the point?" Judi asked.

Meredith closed her book and stroked her new bracelet. "The husband lost interest because Tess, his wife, became boring, mundane."

"How pervasive is cheating—really?" Judi asked.

"Over forty percent of men," Terrie said. "Actually, it's not only men; it's forty percent of people cheat on their spouse."

Judi looked shocked. "It can't be."

Liz furrowed her brow. "Judi, what's with the infidelity questions?"

Meredith took out her compact mirror and looked approvingly at herself. "I know Warren isn't going to ever cheat on *moi*."

"And what's your secret?" Terrie asked.

Meredith placed a twenty on the table. "Gotta go, ladies."

Liz put her hand on Meredith's arm. "Not without telling us."

As she got up to leave, Meredith gave her friends a wry wink and said, "Sex."

CHAPTER 6

After the First Friday meeting, Alex returned to her office to see several more patients. Allowing work to completely distract her from her worries, she proceeded from room to room—until she reached James.

James, a fifteen-year-old boy, was in horrific pain. His mother answered all of Alex's questions while the boy held his neck and looked down at the ground.

"Dr. Rose"—the boy's mother put a hand on her son's shoulder—"we've been dealing with this for six months." She held out three pill bottles. "The doctors have been prescribing medication and nothing has helped."

"I haven't been to PE or my basketball practice in two months, and I can't sleep." The teenager tightened his lips, clearly trying not to get emotional.

Alex went over the different treatments James had tried, including medication, physical therapy, injections, and even psychological counseling. She palpated his spine, and he winced when she touched a few points in his neck. When she performed the Cervical Compression test, putting pressure on his head, his response confirmed the possibility of a cervical disc bulge or herniation.

"He needs an MRI," Alex said.

"None of the physicians on my plan ordered an MRI. And I can't afford to pay for it out-of-pocket," James's mother said.

"He needs one," Alex insisted. She was going to make sure he had an MRI within the next few days even if she had to pay for it herself. She suspected a cervical spine disc bulge or herniation at best and a tumor on the spine at worst; therefore, he definitely required an MRI.

"Aren't you going to adjust him?" The mother put her hands on her hips and looked at Alex, apparently annoyed.

"Definitely not," Alex said. "I am going to call every MRI facility within fifty miles and get him scheduled for one."

"But," the mother started to object, "what do you think is wrong with him?"

"It could be a cervical disc. I'm going to get him in right away, and I'll negotiate a special, hopefully reasonable fee," Alex reassured them. Although she'd worded it as carefully as she could, she knew they were terrified, and she didn't want to tell them she also suspected a tumor. There was no reason to make them even more apprehensive until the diagnosis was confirmed. She promised to get back to them within the next few hours and didn't charge them for the consultation, telling the mother to put it toward the MRI.

She hoped she was wrong about James, but she didn't think so. She really didn't think so. Things like this made her thankful for her wonderful, healthy sons. Tonight, she'd give them each an extra hug.

After finishing at the office, she rushed home.

Daniel was upstairs, busy with his homework, and Jon and Gracie were in the family room playing Connect Four. "Where's your grandma Cecile?" Alex asked Gracie.

"Sleeping in her room," Gracie said. "Grandma Cecile told us she needed fifteen minutes and then she'd be up."

"Does she usually nap?" Alex asked. She'd had no idea Cecile left the children on their own, even for a few minutes. She wanted to go upstairs and ask Cecile, but she thought it might irritate her and probably David too.

When Alex first moved in, she'd suggested they give Cecile's room to Daniel since Cecile wouldn't be needing the room anymore. Wanting to cause as little inconvenience as possible, Alex had thought that would have been a better option instead of converting David's office into a bedroom.

But David didn't want to change Cecile's room, insisting that it would hurt her feelings. The room, like everything in the house, was beautifully appointed, with the two canopy beds, each covered with a soft lilac spread. The top of the white bureau was covered with pictures of Harper: Harper and David, Harper and Gracie, Harper and Warren, all radiant, smiling, happy.

Alex knew Cecile used to sleep over whenever David and Harper went on vacation, and then when Harper got sick, Cecile would stay over and help care for her. After Harper died, Cecile slept at the house whenever David worked late or had to go on a business trip.

Since Gracie was so attached to Cecile, and for that matter, Cecile to Gracie, Alex gladly accepted Cecile's help with transporting her sons as well. But with her practice so far from home, Alex had to depend on Cecile more than she wanted to.

Alex turned to the little girl. "Let's make dinner together, and we'll surprise your daddy."

"No, thank you." Gracie shook her head. "But thank you for asking." Gracie looked away. "Cooking makes me sad 'cause I always did it with my mommy, and now she's not here."

Alex leaned down and put her hands on Gracie's shoulders. "You can help me, and your daddy will be so happy."

Tears welled in Gracie's eyes.

"I have an idea," Alex said. "We could also invite Grandma Cecile."

"Okay."

Alex took out some chicken filets and an egg. She told Gracie to break the egg, then whip it, and then dip the chicken into the egg and then into the flour, praising her all the while.

Eric ran into the house and walked directly to the refrigerator.

"How was practice?" Alex asked.

"Grueling." Eric grabbed an apple from the refrigerator.

Gracie pointed a floured finger at Eric. "I'm cooking Grandma Cecile's dinner, and you can come too."

"Gracie . . ." Alex tousled her hair. "We're a family, and we always eat together."

Eric rolled his eyes.

Gracie looked at Alex. "Are you in my family?"

"Yes," Alex said.

"How come?" Gracie asked.

Alex picked her up and kissed her. "Because I'm your daddy's wife."

"I know, but that doesn't mean you're our family."

Cecile walked into the kitchen, obviously embarrassed about napping. "Sorry, I had a headache and had to lie down for a few minutes. I thought I set the alarm on my phone, but I left it in my car."

"Your phone is here." Jon handed it to her.

"Should I call anyone back?" Cecile asked, obviously confused.

"It didn't ring," Alex said. She worried about Cecile. She was noticeably starting to lose things and was forgetting what time she was supposed to pick up the children. On several occasions, the boys had phoned Alex to tell her Cecile hadn't picked them up. Alex had to call other mothers and beg them to cover for her and pick up the children. When she'd suggested they consider an au pair or another babysitter, David had balked, insisting Cecile was fine.

But Cecile wasn't fine, and Alex knew it.

"Grandma Cecile," Gracie called. "I'm making dinner for you." Gracie held up a piece of floured chicken.

Alex took the battered chicken from Gracie and then turned to Cecile. "Why don't you stay for dinner?"

"I'd best be going home," Cecile said. "My headache."

"Cecile, go up and rest some more and then see if you want some dinner." Alex put more pieces of breaded chicken into the pan.

Gracie ran to her grandmother and wrapped her arms around Cecile's legs. "Grandma, I'll read you a story and you can rest."

Jon, who'd been sitting at the table working on his homework, looked up. "Gracie, you can't read."

"I know all the stories." Gracie put her hands on her hips.

"That's not reading," Jon said.

Gracie turned to follow Cecile upstairs.

Alex called after her. "Gracie, you've got chicken and breadcrumbs on your hands. Come here and wash your hands so you don't get Chicken Love dirty when you see him."

"Chicken Love's a girl. I keep telling you that." Gracie let Alex pick her up to the sink and wash her hands.

An hour later, David returned home. He kissed Alex and asked, "Why's Cecile's car still here?"

"I invited Cecile, and she agreed to stay for dinner," she said, knowing he'd be pleased.

Dinner was wonderful, except when they referred to the chicken as "Gracie's chicken." She'd explained her chicken was Chicken Love and no one should ever eat her Chicken Love.

41

Cecile started to go to the sink. "I enjoyed this so much. Can I do the dishes?"

"Don't be silly. We loved having you," Alex said, although she was even more worried about Cecile now. She'd been so quiet during dinner, apparently having difficulty with the cross-conversation. Yes, there definitely was something that wasn't right, something that was getting worse and worse each day.

As Cecile put on her jacket, she stopped. "I have an idea. Why don't you both do something tomorrow, and let me babysit?"

"Great idea," David said. "We'll play tennis at the club."

"But," Alex said, not sure Cecile could handle getting the boys to their activities while watching Gracie. It would be too much for her.

"Done," David said, and walked Cecile to her car.

When he came back, Alex asked him about the syringes. The syringes in the closet were for Cecile. David explained Cecile needed to inject herself with insulin on a daily basis to control her diabetes, but she kept forgetting to do it. David hadn't hidden them from Alex, he'd just been extra cautious about keeping them away from the children. Alex couldn't have Cecile driving the children if she forgot her insulin. She could pass out while driving, and . . .

CHAPTER 7

On Saturday afternoon, David arranged for them to play tennis at Palisades Tennis Club, the premier club in Orange County. She was thankful it was far away from Brea Tennis Club, the club she and Gabe had joined right after they'd moved to California and had built their social life around club activities. It was also where she'd first met Luke, the man Gabe had set up initially to distract her, then to murder her, the man she'd fallen in love with—no, she hadn't fallen in love; she'd used him to restore the sexuality she thought she'd lost and then he, too, took it away.

But that was the past, she reminded herself as they stopped at the desk to sign in and get their court assignment. Proceeding to the court, David warned Alex, "Don't expect too much. Remember, I went back to the hospital for a caesarian section."

"You look pretty good for a caesarian section," she teased.

They reached the court and introduced themselves to their opponents.

During the warm-up, David seemed to be a little off; his timing wasn't right. But Alex decided she could set him up by hitting some return shots deep to their opponents and that would force them to hit the ball right to David and make him look good at

43

the net. Yes, she was going to send the balls to their opponents fast and low enough so they'd have to pop the balls up and David could slam them down—a hero. And she was going to make sure this evening was about their relationship, which had been overshadowed by their involvement with the children.

David made an excellent shot, and she nodded appreciatively. While David was a good partner, tennis really wasn't his sport. He usually played basketball with the guys at the Jewish Community Center, the facility where Gracie had gone to nursery school. Since Harper wasn't Jewish, they'd agreed to raise Gracie as a Catholic, a promise which David vowed to keep. They'd chosen the Jewish nursery school only for its excellent reputation, not for any religious reason.

David's phone rang. He looked at Alex. "Sorry, I have to take it."

Five minutes later, David returned to the court. Apologizing profusely, he took his place next to her.

When they finished playing, the other couple invited David and Alex to the club's bar for a drink.

"Babysitter," Alex and David said at the same time.

The other couple nodded. The wife said, "Ours is old enough to babysit for his brother."

"Three boys might never be old enough to be left alone," Alex joked.

"And one girl," David said and looked at Alex.

"Gracie," she said, and hoped he didn't think she purposely hadn't mentioned Gracie. She decided he was preoccupied with his phone call. But then she always rationalized; she'd done that for so long with Gabe, and then it was too late. Actually, she realized it had more to do with her not trusting herself. And now, even when everything was different, safe, the memory ghosts sometimes slipped into her life.

They walked to the car.

She asked, "What's going on with the phone?" Since he'd take the call during the match, she knew it had to be important.

"Alex, there's an organization in New York."

"I know you've been going to New York for years."

"This is different," he said, his voice full of passion and conviction. "That was for the gynecology board and—"

"The International Federation of Gynecology and Obstetrics," she said. Yes, he'd already told her about the convention he'd attended in New York on the night Harper died, the night Harper took all of her Ambien tablets at once, and the night she just slipped into the bathtub and was gone.

"Alex, did you hear me?" he asked.

"Sorry," she said, and turned her attention away from things that were in the past, things that shouldn't haunt the present; but they did.

"I wasn't sure I was going to get involved, but they told me how many children are trafficked each year, how much it costs to fund the rescues, and the challenges of raising the necessary funds. At first, I couldn't commit, but then I was haunted. I'd drop Gracie off at school and wonder—was today the day she'd be taken? You can't imagine what's going on in the world—the United States, even in Orange County."

She looked at him, shocked, and asked, "Orange County?"

"Yes," he whispered. "There are sex trafficking rings right here. We have—"

"We," she repeated. "So, you're already committed."

"I have to . . ."

"Why?"

"That's who I am, and you knew it when you met me."

She had to agree. "Okay. Tell me about it."

45

"Child Rescue is . . ."

"Isn't that the organization Ashton Kutcher started?" she asked.

"No," he said. "Kutcher's organization is Thorn. Their motto is, 'We won't stop until every child can be a kid,' and believe me, they won't."

"What's Child Rescue then?"

"According to Child Rescue, two million children are trafficked and exploited annually."

"Two million," she repeated. She knew how horrific sex trafficking was, but the numbers shocked her.

"Yes," he said. "Child Rescue just funded an aftercare orphanage in Cusco, Peru, but they couldn't accommodate all the children who were rescued, so they are being housed in a local jail. A jail."

He continued, "Child Rescue was co-founded by Stephanie Larsen, the first woman in her family in one hundred years who wasn't sexually exploited. I know I have to do whatever I can to protect innocent children."

She looked at him as though seeing his heart, his true heart. Sure, she knew he cared for women in his clinic, went all over the world with the Flying Samaritans, but this was a passion which was beyond that.

Now, she was interested. Child trafficking was a cause which she, actually every parent, had to be passionate about. She couldn't even fathom the pain and agony the children—or for that matter the parents—went through at the hands of a trafficker.

As he spoke about the organization, the passion in his voice was audible, almost contagious: "Children are captured and then placed in shelters where they are kept for men to come in and have sex with them. It's beyond disgusting. They're trafficked at six years—"

She gasped. "Six?" She listened to him for the next twenty minutes and was hooked. "I'm in."

"Alexandra, you're my soul mate."

He'd never called her Alexandra. He sounded so emotional, and she could tell he was truly touched, deeply touched.

"Harper never backed my 'crazy schemes,' as she called them, even the Flying Samaritans. Whenever I went on the Flying Samaritan trips, there was always a fight. When Harper got sick, I completely stopped going. I didn't want to leave her. Then after Harper died, I wanted to be with Gracie as much as possible. But when Cecile offered to take Gracie for some weekends, I decided to go back to the Flying Samaritans, especially since they'd never found another gynecologist."

"Yes. I'm so grateful you did." She smiled. "Or else we never would have met."

"Best thing I ever did, but . . ."

"What?"

"I knew the weekends when I was away, Cecile made sure Gracie got to spend time with her uncle Warren. I hated that, but it made Gracie so happy."

"You and Warren are going to be okay—right? I mean, you do believe he had nothing to do with Harper's death. Right?"

"Yes. No. I'm not sure, but it doesn't matter."

She knew there was still something cutting David to the core, but he took her hand and kissed her finger. "Soul mate," he whispered.

"Soul mate," she said as they pulled up to Las Brisas.

◆◆◆

After a lovely dinner overlooking the ocean, Alex and David returned home. Cecile had just finished putting Gracie to bed and almost started to cry. She couldn't find her keys and was getting agitated.

"We'll find them," David promised, and went to search the family room.

Daniel came downstairs. "Just finished reading to Jon and he's asleep, but I need you to proof this." He handed his report to Alex.

"Thanks for taking care of Jon." Alex was so appreciative of how he took care of his younger brother. She took Daniel's report. "First, we have to help Cecile look for her keys while I—"

"And glasses," Cecile said. "I think I left them in Gracie's room after I read to her."

Eric closed the refrigerator door, turned around, and when Cecile wasn't looking, he slipped Alex a pair of glasses which he'd found on a shelf in the refrigerator.

Giving Eric a conspiratorial nod, Alex took the glasses and put them on the counter. It was uncharacteristically sensitive of Eric, and for that, she was grateful. Obviously, he knew it would have embarrassed Cecile and wanted to save her that. This was a milestone for Eric—a newfound compassion, but it was also gut-wrenching to see Cecile's confusion.

"One set of keys right next to Lucky's leash." Daniel held out the keys.

Cecile reached for the keys. "I was going to take Lucky for a walk."

Obviously shocked, David raised his voice and asked, "And leave Gracie in the house alone?" Up until now, he'd been defending Cecile whenever Alex suggested they find another means of childcare. Despite Cecile's "little episodes of forget-fulness," even to the extent of not picking up the boys when expected, David refused to consider anyone besides Gracie's beloved grandma Cecile—that was, up until now. He was protective of Gracie and couldn't handle any possible carelessness, and leaving Gracie in the house, even with the boys, was not something David would tolerate.

Cecile started to cry. "I . . . I wasn't going to . . ."

"It's okay." David hugged Cecile and walked her out to her car.

Alex knew she and David needed to talk about Cecile, but Daniel was waiting for her to review his report. "Sorry, give me a few minutes to review it," she said to him.

"That's not what I was going to ask about." Daniel looked at his mother. "I think she's in bad shape."

"She's wacko," Eric said, returning to his usual teenage unsympathetic behavior.

"You were really nice to save her from being embarrassed about putting her glasses in the refrigerator." Alex gave Eric a kiss on the forehead and sat down to review Daniel's report.

David came back into the house. "She'll be okay. We're going to make an appointment to get her evaluated by a neurologist."

"I hope so." Alex wanted to believe him, but feared this was just the beginning of what was to become a downward spiral for Cecile.

"I'm going up to check on Gracie." David bent down and kissed Alex's cheek.

"I'll be up soon," she said, and started to read Daniel's paper on *King Lear*. As usual, Daniel's use of language and ability to present his thoughts cohesively and concisely were outstanding. At such a young age, he seemed to understand the pain of the parent-child relationship. He'd even quoted her favorite line from *King Lear:* "How sharper than a serpent's tooth it is to have a thankless child." Yes, he'd done a wonderful job, as always. She corrected just two minor grammatical errors.

She said good night to Daniel and Eric, cautioning them not to stay up too late, and went upstairs to her bedroom.

David was in the shower, and just as she started to undress, she heard Gracie yell, "Mommy."

"David," Alex called, but he obviously didn't hear with the water running.

"I need you, Mommy. Hurry." Gracie's cry seemed urgent.

Alex ran to Gracie's room and said, "Your daddy's in the shower. What can I get for you?"

"I need a real mommy." Gracie was crying and hugging her Chicken Love.

"I love you, Gracie."

"Do you love me like a real mommy?"

"Gracie, of course I do," Alex said, and thought how having a daughter changed you. With sons there was the fear they'd fall or get hurt playing sports; then there was driving. It was terrifying with boys, but not like the fear of sexual abuse at the hands of some sadistic perpetrator, which, she was sure, plagued David. "I love you," Alex repeated.

"Why?" Gracie asked.

"Because you're the most lovable baby girl I know." She looked at Gracie and smiled. She understood David's need to work for Child Rescue and knew if he ever put a face to the abused girls, it was so much more painful. Then the magnitude of the horrific act multiplied a thousandfold. Before, it was just a story, but then it became visceral. And if ever there was a possibility it could happen to your child, that fear took sinister wings.

"I still wish I had a real mother," Gracie said.

Alex hugged Gracie. "I'm real."

"But I still need my daddy to sleep with me."

"I'll get him." Alex went to get David. As soon as she told him what had happened, he rushed to Gracie's room.

She knew he'd come back to bed, and they'd have sex. She mused at how their lovemaking had fallen into a pattern: He'd go check on Gracie and then return to bed, reach for her, kiss her lips, and then, as quickly as he'd initiated it, it was over.

They always wore sexless pajamas—appropriately covered up—just in case one of the children called or came to the room. Their rushed lovemaking also was because David was hesitant about locking the bedroom door. He said it would terrify Gracie if she came to their door and found it locked.

No, tonight was going to be different, she decided.

She jumped out of bed, rushed to the bureau, and grabbed her nightgown—the red one, the one she'd bought years ago but hadn't been able to bring herself to wear ever again. It was the one she'd worn the night she waited in the hotel room for her former husband to return from gambling and celebrate their twentieth wedding anniversary. That was the night she'd thrown the nightgown on the hotel floor at two in the morning and realized he wasn't coming back to make love to her. That was the night she'd feared they'd never make love again, only to learn it was true.

Just as she put on the negligee, David came back to the bedroom.

"Gorgeous," he said, and reached out to her.

"Love you." She leaned into his embrace and inhaled his lemony scent—fresh like the color yellow.

While he held her, she softly stroked his back, then his hair. They kissed with an urgency, as though for the first time. Her breath quickened, and her breasts felt heavy, yearning for his touch. Wanting to hold on to the moment, have it last, they stood at the foot of the bed. Then he lifted her and placed her onto the bed.

51

She watched as he took off his pajama top, then pants. He stood over her, already erect and ready to take her. She wanted him more than she'd ever wanted him before.

He got into bed and kissed her lips, then moved down her body, kissing her breasts and then her belly. He took her breast in his hand and fondled her nipple until she begged for him to climb on top of her.

"Wait," he whispered, and continued to press her nipple between his fingers.

She stroked his penis and then sucked on him until he moaned, "I need you now."

She lay back and opened her legs for him to enter.

He arched his back and looked into her eyes as he came, emitting a groan so guttural she could almost feel it in her body. They came together with an intensity they'd never allowed themselves before this moment. They'd connected, connected in the secret place where no one else knows you except your lover.

She felt safe. Not even Harper's memory could separate them now. She'd always wondered whether he was there with her or far away, wishing for Harper. Tonight, she knew he was hers, always and forever. She didn't wonder what he was thinking, whether he was wishing for Harper; no, she knew he was here with her. And there was no place else in the world she'd rather be than right here in David's embrace.

CHAPTER 8

Although Alex and David were worried about Cecile, they decided they'd wait to hire someone to help with the children. They feared upsetting Cecile and hoped maybe, just maybe, she'd be fine. That's what David would have liked, but they both knew this was more than just a few transient episodes of forgetfulness.

Since David had decided to join the board of Child Rescue, he was packing for his trip to New York. When Alex walked into the bedroom with the clean, starched shirts she'd just picked up on her way home, Gracie and Jon were running around.

David looked up from his suitcase and reached for the shirts. "Perfect. You're the best."

Gracie ran to David and grabbed his leg. "I thought I was your best, and I'm going with you to the apple."

"Gracie girl, I'm trying to pack." David picked his daughter up and kissed her. "And it's the Big Apple. New York."

Gracie pointed to Alex. "Daddy, I don't have to stay with her, do I?"

"You have to mind Alex the whole time I'm gone," he said.

"We'll have a good time here." Alex winked at Gracie. "Let's go downstairs and finish the surprise we're making for your daddy to take to New York."

"I want to stay with you, Daddy, and I don't want you to go if I can't stay with my grandma Cecile like I always do." Gracie started to cry.

David stopped packing and whispered something in Gracie's ear.

After listening to her father, Gracie turned to Alex. "I'll be a very good girl. I promise, 'cause—"

David put his finger to his lips. "Our secret."

"And I have a secret for you too," Alex said.

Jon looked up. "I thought you said secrets were rude."

"Sometimes, there are things we can't share, or sometimes we have a surprise for someone and don't want to ruin it," Alex said, but she also knew how secrets, especially in families, could be dangerous. She looked over toward their bathroom. Yes, the secrets that room held often frightened her. She hated secrets. They took on a life of their own, and sometimes they were more damaging than reality.

"Okay, I have a secret from her." Jon looked at Gracie. Usually these two, "the little ones" as Alex and David had taken to referring to them, were colluding together. They'd become fast friends almost from the moment they met at Meredith and Warren's wedding, when Meredith selected Jon as the ring bearer and Warren insisted Gracie, his beloved niece, be the flower girl. Yes, that also was where Alex and David had reconnected.

They'd first met on the Flying Samaritans' trip to Mexico six months before Meredith and Warren's wedding. On their trip to Guerrero Negro, Alex and David had worked together treating the indigent villagers. They were attracted to each other and had agreed to see each other on the next trip, but Alex had been consumed by her custody battle, and she never went on another trip with the Flying Samaritans.

David continued to go to Guerrero Negro every month, and he later confessed he kept hoping Alex would show up. He could have called her, but he hadn't. He later told her it was too soon after his wife's death to consider dating. But when they saw each other at Meredith and Warren's wedding, it was love at second sight!

Jon patted Lucky, who was nuzzling him. Since his chore was feeding Lucky, it seemed Lucky knew exactly who to go to whenever it was close to feeding time. Alex insisted they all have chores, and this was one he took very seriously and never forgot, especially with Lucky's help.

"Mommy," Jon said, interrupting her thoughts about her first meeting with David.

"What is it?" she asked.

"I can't talk about secrets 'cause I have to do my responsibility for Lucky." He scampered downstairs.

Gracie reached for her dad's hand and looked up at him. "I told you I will behave good, but I'm not going to call her Mommy."

"Of course not," Alex reassured Gracie. She and David had decided it was too soon for Gracie to even think about calling her Mommy anyway. They'd talked about how they were going to gently suggest it in time. But Alex knew plans were sometimes so much easier than reality and timing was as important as—no, sometimes it was even more important than the details.

Alex nodded at Gracie, reminding her she was supposed to finish drawing the surprise Valentine's card for her dad. Alex had told her she was going to slip it into his suitcase since he wouldn't be home to celebrate.

"Gracie," she said. "Let's go downstairs and make dinner."

"Sure," Gracie said. "That's a great idea."

David looked surprised but pleased.

While Alex prepared the chicken, Gracie worked on the card. Then she handed it to Alex and asked, "Can I do the cooking now?"

"Of course," Alex said, and told her to put the sauce and then a slice of mozzarella on each piece of chicken.

Eager to get to a basketball game at his school, Eric set the table and poured water into all of the glasses.

Daniel made the salad, his "specialty," as he referred to it. He actually was quite a good cook, and when Alex was stuck at the office, she'd talk him through various recipes on her way home from work.

Jon came into the kitchen, and when he saw Gracie working with Alex, he scrunched up his nose. "Why's Gracie doing my job?"

Alex handed him the grated parmesan cheese. "You can follow Gracie and put this cheese on the chicken, and then I'll put it onto the pasta plate, and—"

"Do we have to have a ceremony over this cooking?" Eric asked. "I want to get out of here tonight. We have a basketball game at school and then—"

"You will have a family dinner first," Alex said. She was pleased he'd made friends at his new school, not an easy task for a sophomore in high school. But he needed to know family dinners were important also. Then she asked him about his homework.

"I did my homework," Eric said. "Daniel isn't the only one pulling perfect grades here."

"So proud of you." Alex hugged him. They'd been getting along better than ever. True, he missed his father, but lately, he didn't seem to be pulled by Gabe's negative comments about her.

After dinner and playing several rounds of Connect Four, David said, "Gracie girl, your Chicken Love is in bed waiting for you. Time to go to bed."

"I can bring Chicken Love downstairs," Gracie offered.

"Time," David repeated, and as he did every night he was home, he walked her upstairs and read to her.

A half hour later, Alex signaled to Jon. "Your turn."

"Mommy," he said. "Can I have a story even though I can read now?"

"Why don't you read to me?" she asked.

"No, I'm too tired to work right now," he said. He was still her funny, sweet baby even though he was seven. With the other boys so much older and independent, Alex relished time with her baby. And although Eric considered Jon an annoyance, Daniel was always ready to help his younger brother and often played games with him.

Alex got under the covers with Jon. "Tell me what you liked best about the week," she said.

"I liked when Danny played ball with me. That made me win on my team."

"Didn't you like when we all cheered for you at your game?"

"No," he reminded her. "My daddy wasn't there."

"But you played so well." She knew he missed his father. Yes, she also knew no matter what cruel act a parent committed, the child still yearned for their approval. She knew that all too well. Yes, even when her mother snubbed out the burning cigarette on Alex's wrist, she needed to believe it was an accident or else the world was unsafe, and she had to be cautious, very cautious.

Jon scrunched up his nose. "Since I was so good, would you read to me?"

She read him a story, the biography of Alexander Hamilton, an orphan. He asked whether Gracie was an orphan since she didn't have a mother. Alex explained how Gracie had her father, and now she had a whole family to love her.

Alex shut the door to Jon's room and started toward her bedroom.

David was just closing his suitcase when she walked in. "If I forgot anything, then I don't need it."

"Me. You're forgetting to take me." She walked up to him and hugged him.

He turned to her, kissed her, and pulled her close.

She could feel his heart beat against hers.

He locked the door.

"You're locking the door?" she said, surprised since this was the first time he'd ever done that.

"Alex, I'm not going to let you out until I have you."

They made love, gentle love, the lovemaking she and David had grown accustomed to. Amazing how sex was completely different with each lover—like the act was reinvented and the pattern was different for each couple.

Afterwards, he got up and unlocked the door. "Be right back."

He didn't return to the bed for an hour. She feared something was wrong. She even imagined he felt guilty after they made love, here in Harper's bed. He'd walk around the house, and once she'd found him staring at an album with pictures of Harper.

When he finally returned to bed, she asked, "Are we living in the past or the present?" True, death wasn't the same as deception, but it was there like an albatross in their lives. Every time she ran her fingers along the cold porcelain bathtub, Harper was there.

"Alex, we are our past. That's what makes us who we are. You're stronger because Gabe left you, and you had to become a different person. I'm who I am because, in a sense, Harper left me too. I was on automatic and then life became precious, tenuous—every day was—"

"What really happened to Harper?" she asked. There had to be something, some secret that David hadn't told her. It was the way he'd truncate any conversation about how Harper died that made her uneasy. Now, Alex decided she had to know.

"I don't know if it was suicide."

She stared at him. There, he'd said it. There it was. He could never take it back. Her horrific fear was realized. "You killed her?" There, she'd said it. The parasite that had been living within her was released.

"I would never kill my wife."

"Wife," Alex whispered. He still referred to Harper as his wife. How could he look at her and utter the word *wife* for another?

"What happened? You can tell me. I won't tell anyone." Maybe he, too, was a monster like her former husband and would morph into one right before her eyes. "Tell me," she cried out, forgetting about the children, forgetting about how much she loved him, fearing the worst and ready to believe anything.

"I think Warren—"

"What are you even saying? Why didn't you go to the police if you suspected him?" There was something—a look in his eyes. She'd never seen it before. Maybe it had been there all along, and she'd never noticed. Could she have slipped into another marriage with a man just like Gabe? Her heart was pounding. There was a truth she was going to hear. She hoped this truth wasn't going to be ugly enough, terrifying enough, powerful enough to ruin their family.

"Alex, you're looking at me and making up a story in your head, but you're wrong."

"Then tell me exactly what happened," she demanded.

"I was in New York for a meeting. Harper was weak, so her mother took Gracie for the day and then kept her for the night. I offered to come home, but she said it wasn't necessary, and I couldn't do anything anyway. I changed my flight, anyway, and got out as soon as possible."

"So, you were here?" she asked.

"No," he said. "Harper wanted to take Laetrile, and I refused . . ."

Even though she'd heard about the Laetrile from Meredith, Alex was shocked. "You wouldn't pay for the Laetrile?"

He sat on the bed and leaned his head on his hand. "Alex, you have to know I would have paid for anything, but she insisted on stopping all her chemotherapy. I think Warren was going to take her to Mexico to some clinic that did intravenous—"

"How do you know?"

"We'd argued about it. And after she died, I realized she'd withdrawn a hundred thousand dollars from our account. I knew her brother Warren . . ."

"You think Warren?" Surprised, she looked at him. He couldn't think Warren would have killed his sister for a hundred thousand or, for that matter, any amount. True, Warren was ostentatious and his gifts to Meredith were proof of that, but according to Meredith, he absolutely adored Harper, and he and his sister were each other's closest friend.

"Alex, there's more. After Harper's death, I studied all the bank statements for the first time. I mean, I'd glance at them before, but even when she was so sick, right up until her death, Harper took care of all our financials."

"What does financial stuff have to do with her death?" Alex asked. She and everyone in Laguna Beach knew about Harper, the sought-after interior designer and real estate investor who'd made her fortune flipping houses, expensive houses, but she couldn't understand why he was bringing this up instead of talking about what really happened. "I don't get it," she said when he didn't answer her.

"Whenever I'd ask Harper about some withdrawals from our account, she'd tell me she had to loan money to Warren. She'd tell me something about his deals not funding properly, and he only needed the money for a short time. But the withdrawals kept getting more significant."

"Warren," she whispered, as though saying his name softly would erase any evil. Alex knew this would destroy Meredith. She'd been so happy with Warren. Always showing off the jewels he'd bought her. Always bragging about places he'd take her. She was shocked but didn't want to show it, for fear he would stop talking, and she had to hear the truth, David's truth.

It didn't make sense, and she asked, "David, why wouldn't you say anything?"

"I'm not sure what happened. All I had was a dead wife and a deadbeat brother-in-law. Gracie needed her grandma Cecile; she was the only other person Gracie had. I'd never take a chance of losing her grandmother."

"She wouldn't lose her grandmother," Alex said.

"Oh, you don't know Cecile. Her family can do no wrong. And I had no proof. I couldn't chance it. It wouldn't bring Harper back anyway."

"Did you really find her in the bathtub?"

"Warren did. And when they did the autopsy, they found she'd taken enough Ambien to put a three-hundred-pound man to sleep, and—"

"David, I still don't see the connection between Warren and her death."

"My torturous and horrific thought is that Warren saw his loans were going to end once Harper died, so he wanted to be sure he got enough out of her beforehand. Maybe that was why he'd told her about the clinic in Mexico where she could get Laetrile infusions, and she had to pay cash."

"Are infusions that much?" she asked. Although she'd known about the Laetrile from Meredith, she had no idea about the clinic in Mexico. And she also knew the real problem for David had been Harper's refusal to continue with conventional medication in favor of the Laetrile, and David blamed Warren for that.

"Alex, I have no idea what that crap costs, but I do know she could have had a few more months, just a few . . ." He teared up.

"But why would you even think Warren would make up a story about a clinic?"

"Alex, I told you—money. And when they did the autopsy, they found a high level of alcohol in her system, and . . ."

Alex was trying to process, but it wasn't making sense; there was more, much more. Maybe, she thought, Harper, fabulous, incredibly successful Harper, could have been an alcoholic. Yes, alcoholism and drugs were rampant, even in pristine, luxurious homes. "And?" she asked.

"The only time she'd have a drink was with Warren. They'd always have a glass of wine. After she got sick, she was told to stay away from alcohol, but she said it would make her forget she was sick for a while, and she and Warren . . ."

He looked away and clenched his jaw. "In my craziness, I've thought maybe Warren put the Ambien in her wineglass, gave it to her, and . . ."

"You think Warren . . ." She stared at him.

"Alex, it's been tormenting me for two years. Two years."

"But what's the thing with going to Mexico with him for Laetrile?"

"To get her to give him money."

"Are you sure?"

"Her suitcase was in the bedroom closet. Packed."

CHAPTER 9

Alex tossed and turned all night. After David had shared the truth with her—or what he thought was the truth—behind Harper's death, Alex decided she had to call Liz. The things David had said last night just didn't make sense, and Liz would know what she should do.

Liz suggested they meet for dinner, insisting she owed Alex a belated birthday celebration and now was the perfect time, especially since David had gone to New York. At first Alex refused to go, stating she couldn't leave the children home.

"What about Cecile?" Liz asked.

"She just stopped driving at night." Actually, Alex thought, Cecile shouldn't be driving at all; her confusion seemed to be escalating. But Cecile did offer to come over every night that David was in New York and put Gracie to bed. Cecile told Alex she would Uber to their house. Alex thought she was waiting for an invitation to stay over and sleep in her bedroom, the room David refused to change.

"Alex, you can give up the Super Mom thing for one night."

"Okay," Alex said. "If Cecile agrees."

Cecile was delighted, and as Alex had predicted, Cecile offered to sleep over, stating how convenient it would be to go to church

63

with Gracie in the morning. Alex told her that wasn't necessary since she wouldn't be home late. Then, upon seeing the disappointment in Cecile's face, she agreed it would be easier if she stayed the night, and it definitely would be a treat for Gracie.

Just as Alex was putting on her earrings, Jon walked into the bedroom. "Lucky's been a good girl all day, so I want to take her for a walk." He held up her leash.

"No," Alex said. "You can just let her out in the backyard and run with her." Although Laguna Beach was supposedly as safe as Brea, Alex wasn't comfortable letting Jon take Lucky out alone. In Brea, they'd known everyone on the block, and he'd always just gone to the end of the cul-de-sac. Alex never worried about the boys playing outside. Here, it seemed everyone was always inside their houses or in their backyard, where they wouldn't hear anything. None of the children played in the street. And the coyotes from the hillside often roamed the neighborhood. Maybe she was being overly vigilant, but she had to protect the boys. She couldn't take any chances; she couldn't be too cautious.

"We'll both take a long walk with her tomorrow," Alex promised.

◆◆◆

Seasons 52, known for the best happy hour in Orange County, was packed. So, Alex thought, this was where people went when they had no children waiting for them at home, no children who'd tell them about the triumphs and injustices of the day, and no one for whom they'd make dinner, draw baths, help with homework, read a story, and kiss good night.

Liz was already seated at a table in the bar, drink in hand, studying the menu.

Alex leaned over and kissed her cheek. "If you were Meredith, you'd be surveying the bar to see which man was admiring you."

"Yeah, they're all looking over here," Liz teased. She certainly wasn't a woman that a man would check out. Her hair was a little thin, her nose a little too long, but her skin was perfect, unlined, almost radiant—especially for a forty-five-year-old. Her lipstick had most probably disappeared at lunch, and she'd neglected to reapply it—so unlike Meredith.

"Babe, how've you been?" Liz asked.

"Needing this." Alex pointed to Liz's cocktail.

Liz took a sip. "The lamb chop lollipops are their happy hour specialty."

Alex closed her menu. "I wouldn't know. My usual happy hour is convincing Gracie macaroni and cheese is not a gourmet delicacy."

"How's it going with Gracie?" Liz asked.

Before Alex could answer, the waiter came over and took their orders. Liz selected the lamb lollipops, and Alex decided on the scallops on a bed of cabbage and a pomegranate martini.

Ordering complete, Liz handed Alex her birthday card and a beautifully wrapped box. "Belated birthday gift."

The card, affirming Liz's gratitude for the years of friendship, touched Alex, but in reality, it was she who had been the recipient of Liz's support over the past three turbulent years. "Love you," Alex said, and opened her gift. The cashmere scarf was perfect: pink, gray, and white. It was soft and would match Alex's sweaters, mostly grays and blacks. As Alex wrapped the scarf around her neck, it snagged on one of her earrings, the earrings David had given her, the earrings she feared had belonged to Harper.

"Thank you so much," Alex said.

"I asked about Gracie," Liz reminded Alex. "I mean, according to Meredith, she really knows how to manipulate her uncle Warren and supposedly has him totally wrapped around her finger."

"Warren," Alex repeated.

The waiter delivered their orders.

Alex moved to the side as he placed her plate in front of her. "Liz, I don't know if I can tell you, but . . ."

Liz took a sip of her cocktail. "You know the First Friday Book Club's rule is no secrets."

"Yes, and it appears that the exact reverse is happening." Alex started to cry. "I'm so confused I can't think."

Liz leaned across the table and took Alex's hand. She didn't speak; she didn't need to. Alex knew from her look that she was safe.

Alex nodded. "I . . . Well, David said Harper had been giving Warren money through the years, and . . ."

Liz put down her lamb chop. "That slime. I thought, according to Meredith, he does so well."

"Actually, David told me Harper had given Warren thousands. But once Meredith came into his life, he started 'borrowing' even more."

"So, all her fancy jewelry . . ." Liz sipped her drink.

"David didn't actually say why, but he hinted that Warren wasn't doing as well as we all thought." Alex shook her head. "I don't know. Meredith is really sharp, and I can't imagine her missing this."

"We all miss things when we're in love." Liz took a bite of her lamb lollipop.

"Don't I know it," Alex said.

"I wasn't criticizing you."

"I know." Alex took a sip of her cocktail. She did know Liz, although acerbic at times, had never been critical of her. And Alex thought this suspicion might be unfounded. "But Harper withdrew a hundred thousand dollars a week before she died, and David suspects she gave it to Warren for some clinic in Mexico."

Liz shook her head. "Do you think any clinic in Mexico would cost that much?"

"How do I know?" Alex asked. "David said he and Harper had arguments about her wanting to take Laetrile like Meredith said, but . . ." She took a breath. "David did find a packed suitcase in her closet."

"Still seems far-fetched," Liz said. "And why would he kill her if she kept giving him money?"

Alex put down her fork. "Or he knew it was going to end when she died so . . ."

Liz pointed her lamp chop lollipop at Alex. "It does make sense; that is, if Warren is really a terrible, mercenary man."

"Okay," Alex said, "Here's the thing, David said they found Ambien . . ."

Liz nodded. "It was in the news—and alcohol. Everyone heard that one."

"David told me he thought Warren put the Ambien in her glass and . . ."

"Proof? Alex, what proof?"

"None," Alex said. "It's horrific, but I have to confess, for me, it feels better than thinking David . . ."

"Alex, you never told me you suspected David of anything."

"I didn't even want to think it, much less say it." Alex hadn't wanted to face her deepest fear, her fear that David had killed his wife and she'd married another man who appeared nice and caring but was, in reality, just the opposite. Alex touched the scar on her right wrist, knowing only too well, reality was whatever story a person made up about an event, especially a critical one.

They discussed the pros and cons of telling Meredith and decided against it for now, just for now. Then Alex looked at her watch. "Cecile is watching the kids, and I don't want to take advantage."

"Is her husband alive?" Liz asked.

"He died three years ago, right before Harper was diagnosed."

"Warren must have gotten money when his father died."

"No, I think their father left everything to Cecile." Alex pushed her plate away. "And he probably thought, like everyone, that Warren was doing so well. He certainly knew Harper didn't need anything."

"That's it then," Liz said. "Warren must have thought he was going to come into a lot of money and then when he didn't . . ."

Alex nodded. "Poor Cecile. Her daughter died a year after her husband. Gracie became her world. And now that Warren's married to Meredith, I'm sure he doesn't have much time to spend with his mother."

"Yep, our Meredith can be a handful."

She kissed Liz and drove home to find Cecile had managed beautifully.

Alex went upstairs to check on Jon. Just as she was ready to walk out of the room, he called to her. "What about my questions?"

Every night she would ask him questions about the best and worst part of the day. They'd go over the day. She knew sometimes the little things built up, and then before you knew it, a person became different: angry, unhappy, even evil. She wanted to make sure he went to sleep with only positive thoughts. She had to dispel all negativity, protect him as much as possible. She smiled at him. "Jon, we'll do the questions longer tomorrow."

"That's not fair."

"I love you. Good night," she said. *Fair, life isn't fair.*

She went downstairs and thanked Cecile again. Recently, Cecile was so much more accepting of her. The only issue was Cecile's constant insistence on Warren's presence at family events and her disappointment when David refused. But David did agree to have everyone over to celebrate Cecile's seventieth birthday next weekend, insisting it would be once, just once.

CHAPTER 10

While David was upstairs unpacking from his trip to New York, Alex prepared for their first dinner in the formal dining room. The silverware, dishes, glasses, all parts of their past blending together, were arranged atop place mats on the glistening mahogany table. David had told her the story of how cleverly Harper had ferreted out the table at an estate sale. It seemed as hard as David tried to hold on to his past, she tried just as hard to forget hers. Yes, they both had memory ghosts, and his were to hold while hers were to forget.

After she set the table and put the place cards down, careful not to put Warren next to David, she turned on the light and smiled. The table actually glistened under the light; it was perfect, magical. She decided she'd start a tradition of eating in the dining room for birthdays and holidays.

Alex looked at her watch and rushed upstairs to change.

Just as she was zipping her dress, Gracie ran into their room and asked Alex to help her put a bow in her hair—a sign the week together was a success. Gracie was willing to have Alex help her with so much more than before. And when Alex did help, Gracie was genuinely appreciative.

"Thank you," Gracie said, and scampered off to play Connect Four with Jon.

As David was shaving, he called to Alex. "I think this was a bad idea."

Alex turned and put her arms around his waist. "It'll be fine."

"Remind me again, why are we doing this?" David asked, uncharacteristically annoyed.

"Because it's Cecile's birthday, because she's Gracie's grandma and her favorite person in the world—except for you. Oh, and because Meredith doesn't cook."

"Um."

"Come on, you and Warren can be civil for one evening."

"That's what you think," David said.

Ever since David had told her of his suspicion about Warren extricating money from Harper and his possible involvement in her death, Alex was more understanding of the dissension between the two men.

The doorbell rang.

"My grandma's here," Gracie called from Jon's room, and ran downstairs to open the door.

Jon, Alex, and David followed.

As soon as Cecile came into the house, Gracie blurted out, "I know what my daddy got you for your birthday."

Alex put her finger to her lips. "Sweetie, it's supposed to be a surprise."

Cecile laughed and bent down to kiss Gracie. Then Cecile walked into the foyer. As she passed the dining room and saw the table, she turned to Alex and said, "I don't know why you had to go to so much trouble for this dinner."

"Our pleasure." Alex reached for Cecile's coat. The original plan had been for a huge seventieth birthday party, held at the Ritz

71

and hosted by Warren. Cecile refused, insisting she only wanted her family around her—most probably referring only to Warren and Gracie. But since Meredith didn't cook, Alex had offered.

Cecile patted Jon on the head. "Hello, honey."

"No, I'm not Honey." Jon frowned. "I miss my Honey so much. She was the best dog in the world, but she died."

"You look lovely," Cecile said when Alex returned from putting her coat away.

"And you could pass for forty," David said as he walked into the room.

Cecile was a pretty woman. She did look like the pictures Alex had seen of Harper, only older. She had an ethereal look about her, maybe because she'd faced death, first her husband's, then her daughter's, and knew how close it was. When she smiled, her eyes sparkled. They were blue, almost aquamarine, a feature Harper, Warren, and Gracie all shared, but Gracie's were the bluest of them all. Cecile's eyes were one of her best features, along with her long white hair, which, although it did age her, was thick, healthy—healthier than she was.

David and Cecile went into the family room and started talking about New York. Then Alex heard Cecile suddenly stop midsentence. She'd been doing that more and more. Sometimes, she'd be involved in the conversation, right there, and other times she was lost, almost as though she was daydreaming.

Alex's cell phone rang. It was Meredith calling to say she and Warren were on their way and asking whether Alex needed anything else.

Alex covered the phone and asked David if they needed anything.

David walked to the hallway and whispered, "Yeah, to get this over with."

Eric came downstairs, greeted Cecile, and then followed Alex to the kitchen. "How long do I have to stay?"

"Why?" Alex asked.

"My friend Mark invited me to hang out at his house with some guys from the team." An athlete, Eric was on the basketball team, and he'd made friends almost from the moment they moved to Laguna. Some of his friends were older, and they were already driving at sixteen, but they weren't allowed to have another teenager in the car with them until they were seventeen. After negotiating, Alex agreed he could leave to go to his friend's house, on the condition that he help her serve dinner tonight.

Eric took the baked Brie into the family room just as Daniel was coming downstairs.

Daniel walked over and gave Cecile a hug. "Can I interview you?" he asked.

Cecile looked surprised. "Me?"

Daniel nodded. "We have a section in health class on aging, and . . ."

"I guess I qualify." Cecile laughed.

Daniel asked her a few questions while David poured himself a scotch. He rarely had hard liquor at home. Sure, they'd sometimes have wine with dinner, but he'd never have more than a glass.

The doorbell rang, and Gracie yelled, "Yay. It's my bestest uncle Warren."

Alex took Meredith's coat—Chanel, of course: navy cashmere with a fox collar, elegant and expensive. "Nice," she said.

"Christmas gift," Warren said.

"One of many, I'm sure," Alex said, recalling the purse Meredith had flaunted at the First Friday meeting.

Warren swooped Gracie up in his arms and twirled her. "I spoil my girls."

Alex and David shared a glance; it wasn't supposed to have been a suspicious look, but it was.

David shook hands with Warren. Alex thought it was a good sign.

"Let's have appetizers in the family room first," she said.

They all went into the family room, where they spent the next few awkward moments with no one knowing where to stand or sit, especially David and Warren, who seemed to shift positions so as to avoid each other. Sensing the discomfort, Alex called everyone to the dining room.

Cecile motioned for them all to gather round the table and hold hands.

Alex looked at David, who shrugged. Then he asked Cecile, "Should we really do the prayer thing?"

"Well, we always did. I mean, we are Catholic," Warren said, defending his mother.

"I know that, but . . ." David motioned to Alex and her boys.

"You were always okay with us praying when you were with Harper," Warren said, a bit too hostile for Alex's liking.

"I love traditions," Meredith said. "Let's do it."

Warren led them in a prayer for health, peace, and prosperity. He said a blessing for his mother on her seventieth birthday. He then added a special blessing for his sister, Harper.

"Amen," David said, a peace offering to Warren, an attempt to show Cecile he was respectful of her daughter's memory. It was as though he needed to show her even though he'd remarried, he still honored Harper's memory, Harper's tradition, and his promise that Harper's religion would be preserved for Gracie.

As David took his seat at the head of the table, Jon yelled, "No!" and started to cry.

"What's the matter?" Alex asked.

"If he takes the daddy chair, then we'll never get my daddy back."

Eric shook his head. "Jon always does that whenever we have company."

"He only did it once before," Alex said, defending Jon. But Eric was correct, Jon had done the same thing when she'd invited Luke, her former boyfriend, over for dinner. Cognizant of Jon's reaction to the time Luke took the chair at the head of the table, she'd made certain when they first moved into the house, it was imperative that Jon understand where everyone would sit. But that was at the kitchen table. Things had been going so well for the past few months; therefore, Alex hadn't thought she needed to forewarn him about the seating arrangement in the dining room. She also knew children, no matter how old, never got used to their parents with other partners.

Alex went over to Jon and put her hands on his shoulders. "Jon, be polite. This is David's house, and—"

"Alex, it's your house too," David interrupted.

"I need my daddy." Jon ran upstairs to his room.

Alex got up.

"Should you run to him?" Meredith asked.

"Meredith, are you really the expert on childrearing?" Warren asked, a little sarcastically, which surprised Alex, who excused herself and went upstairs to Jon.

As Alex was walking up the stairs, she heard Meredith say, "We do have two cats, you know."

Within five minutes, Alex and Jon came back downstairs and took their seats at the dining room table as though nothing had happened, but it had. Sometimes, when families were blending, the littlest thing could cause chaos, but that was also the way all families were. It took so much to make it work, but when it did, it was magical, just like tonight, Alex thought as she looked at everyone seated at their beautiful table.

CHAPTER 11

David had prepared the filet mignon for everyone except Jon and Gracie, who had "David's Delicious Hamburgers." Although Gracie begged for macaroni and cheese, she accepted the hamburger, drowned it in ketchup, and ate it all.

Alex had prepared her specialties—fried cauliflower drizzled with cheese, sautéed sweet onions, and twice-baked potatoes. Meredith took a morsel of each of the side dishes. "Alex, you're trying to make me gain weight. Soon, I'll be able to borrow Terrie's peasant blouses and full skirts."

Alex laughed. "That will be the day, Meredith dressed like a flower child of the sixties."

"Do I know Terrie?" Cecile looked confused. Lately, this concerned Alex since ordinary conversations seemed so difficult for her to follow.

After dinner, David brought the remaining plates into the kitchen and handed them to Alex, who was standing at the sink. The boys had been excused. Eric was picked up by his friend's mother, Daniel went to the family room to do some homework, and Jon scampered upstairs to play a computer game. Meredith offered to accompany Cecile upstairs to read Gracie a story before bed. Obviously uncomfortable with Meredith's offer, Cecile agreed nonetheless.

Warren walked into the kitchen and pulled David aside. "I need to talk to you."

"Let's not. There will be words we'll regret," David said.

"It's not what it seems." Warren looked at Alex. "Can we go outside?"

"We're staying right here," David insisted. "And Warren, I know what happened."

"No. You don't. Harper begged me."

"Warren, what are you talking about? I know she gave you money for the Laetrile when I refused."

Alex shut off the faucet and waited for Warren's response.

"David, you have to listen to me," Warren implored.

"I don't have to listen to anything you say."

As though he didn't hear him, Warren continued, "She wanted to die before she became a burden to you, before she lost her dignity. She begged me to help her do it."

"Right."

"She made a bubble bath so I wouldn't see her naked. Then she had me wait until she got in. She wanted me there with her. She knew killing herself was a mortal sin, but she didn't want to live like that, and she knew you'd never allow her to do it."

"No, Warren, I couldn't ever kill my wife, you heartless—"

"My sister begged me for two months. She would cry every time I saw her. She pleaded. I couldn't turn my back on her."

"Warren, did she beg you to take the one hundred thousand dollars she withdrew from our account too?"

"We were going to go to Mexico when you were in New York, but she was too weak, and—"

"And soon after that, you went and bought Meredith that ridiculous ring."

"Don't go there. I would never. If you think I'd kill my sister for money, you're a monster."

"One of us is," David said.

"David, it's not what you think."

"What should I think?" David asked. "A dead wife, thousands of dollars withdrawn from our accounts—a little too easy. What other explanation would you like to offer?"

"I can't," Warren said.

David grabbed Warren by the shirt and held him up against the wall. He slammed his head into the wall. "I could kill you."

She'd never seen David even raise his voice. *Was he this monster or was he just exceedingly angry?* She rubbed her wrist. David's anger was familiar, too familiar.

"Warren, you got her to take out money for Laetrile and then you . . ." David walked outside to the patio. Warren followed and shut the door.

Jon came into the kitchen with Meredith and Cecile.

"Where are Warren and David?" Cecile asked.

"Outside," Alex said, surprised they didn't hear the arguing.

Cecile looked through the glass door, squinting to try to see Warren.

Meredith pursed her lips. "See how domestic I've become. Gracie actually gave *moi* a kiss."

Cecile walked over to the sink. "I'll finish the dishes while you put Jon to sleep if you want."

"Thanks. If Jon stays up too late, then he'll be cranky, and his basketball game is tomorrow."

"I'm never cranky," Jon said.

Alex laughed. "Upstairs with you." She took his hand and walked past the family room, stopping to ask Daniel, "Please come up with me."

Daniel didn't lift his nose from his book. "Reading," he said.

"Daniel, I need you to do me a big favor."

"Whatever," Daniel said, closed his book, and followed her and Jon upstairs.

Once they got upstairs, Alex said, "Danny, please read a story to Jon."

"Mommy, I want you to read to me."

"I have a tummy ache and need to rest," Alex said.

Jon looked panic-stricken. "Are you going to die like Gracie's mom?"

"No, of course not, but I need a few minutes," Alex said. "Will you do Mommy a favor and let Daniel read to you?"

"Okay, if you don't die."

Daniel took Jon to his bedroom, and Alex went down the hall. She walked into her bedroom and closed the door behind her. Then she opened the balcony door and stood in the doorway, where she could hear the men arguing.

"I told you, Harper couldn't take the pain. She knew you'd pump her up with morphine. She didn't want to be kept comfortable, waiting—"

"What's wrong with that?" David yelled.

"I've always taken care of my sister."

"My wife. She was my wife, you—"

"David, it's not what it seems."

"You already said that. Talk and talk fast. I don't know why I didn't go to the police right away. I knew you did it. I couldn't destroy all of Gracie's world."

"My sister did take money out, but only a portion of it was for the Laetrile infusion treatment she was supposed to have that weekend, and another part was used for something, but I can't tell you what."

"You better . . ."

"Um." Warren cleared his throat. "She had an investment, a bad property. Just because my sister had a master's from Harvard doesn't mean she didn't make mistakes." Warren cleared his throat again. "She thought it was a good property, but they kept demanding more money, and . . ."

There was a knock on the bedroom door. "Are you okay?" Meredith asked.

Alex opened the door. "I started to feel sick."

Meredith walked into the bedroom. "What's going on? The guys are outside, you're in here, and I'm stuck with Cecile." She put her hands on her hips and pursed her lips. "Wait, were you listening to the guys?"

"Let's go downstairs," Alex said.

"No, let's talk now," Meredith said. "What did you hear?"

"Exactly what you said at the First Friday Book Club. They were arguing about Warren helping Harper get Laetrile." Well, it wasn't exactly; Alex had left out the part about David suspecting Warren of taking money.

"Okay," Meredith agreed. "Let's get the guys. I've had too much time with Cecile for my liking."

"She's growing on me," Alex said. "I actually like her."

"You want her?"

"I kind of think I already have her," sighed Alex.

When Alex and Meredith got downstairs, Cecile was putting a few of the sterling silver forks and spoons in the garbage.

"What are you doing?" Alex grabbed the silverware out of the garbage.

"I'm cleaning up." Cecile turned back to the sink and continued washing the dishes.

Meredith walked to the sliding glass door and opened it. "Time to go," she called.

Cecile started looking all over the kitchen. "I have to get my car keys."

"You took an Uber." Meredith rolled her eyes. "And we agreed we'd take you home. Remember?"

Warren and David came back into the house.

Alex looked at David and asked, "Is something wrong?"

"Couldn't be better." David smiled, a smile Alex knew meant trouble.

CHAPTER 12

As soon as Meredith, Warren, and Cecile left, Alex checked the garbage pail, making sure Cecile hadn't thrown any other silverware in the trash.

"What are you doing?" David stared at her going through the garbage.

She was going to tell him about Cecile's behavior tonight, how she'd just thrown some silverware into the garbage can and forgotten she hadn't driven herself to their home and was searching for her keys. But first, she wanted to know what had transpired between David and Warren. "Do you want to talk about your conversation with Warren?"

"Tomorrow. I've got two hysterectomies to perform early in the morning." He looked at her. "You look upset. What is it?"

"We can't depend on Cecile," Alex said tentatively, certain he had to have noticed Cecile's confusion tonight. Her difficulty carrying on a conversation was more apparent than ever, and she'd appeared frustrated, especially when two were talking at the same time.

"Alex, I could be here in an instant if—"

"What if you're in surgery? And I'm over an hour away in traffic. We can't have Cecile driving the children." She had no doubt he recognized Cecile's decline, but he wasn't ready to have anyone else care for Gracie.

"Alex, Cecile would be so hurt if we told her she couldn't watch Gracie. Gracie is her life." He turned away, clearly not willing to agree to finding someone else, not just yet. "Besides, when she takes her insulin, she's fine."

"I disagree," she said softly, knowing he probably thought only Cecile could truly empathize with Gracie, understand her Harper-less world.

"I refuse to upset her when she's still trying to cope with the loss of her daughter."

"But our kids could be in danger," Alex said.

David turned to walk upstairs. "It would kill her." Then he mumbled, "And Gracie."

For the next two days, they avoided each other. Like a well-choreographed dance, he'd be in the kitchen when she was in the family room, then they'd change positions, careful to avoid eye contact.

Three days later, the decision was made.

David's cell phone rang late at night. "I'll be right there," he promised.

"What is it?" Alex asked.

David bolted out of bed and hurriedly dressed between clipped one-word sentences: "Warren. Cecile. Hospital. Forgot insulin."

When he left, Alex called Meredith, who explained Cecile had pressed her alert button, and the paramedics arrived at her house within fifteen minutes. Warren also was alerted. The paramedics had transported Cecile to Hoag Hospital, where she was admitted, and Warren rushed to the hospital to be with her.

Alex asked, "How bad is it?"

"Not sure," Meredith replied. "But you don't have to worry about picking Gracie up from school."

Alex couldn't even think about her needs when Cecile could be in critical condition. True, she and David had been depending on Cecile in the afternoons. After school, Cecile would pick up Gracie. If the boys couldn't get a ride, Cecile would often take them to after-school activities—that was, when she remembered.

"Well," Meredith said and paused. "Warren had been picking up Gracie and covering for Cecile whenever she had a headache or felt too dizzy to drive. They'd both go together."

"But I can't believe Gracie wouldn't tell her daddy," Alex said.

"Cecile didn't want David to know because he wouldn't have allowed Warren to be that involved." Meredith took a deep breath. "Warren and Gracie have a special relationship. And if he told her not to say anything, I'm sure she wouldn't. He'd pick her up at least once a week. He made her promise not to tell anyone she was with her uncle Warren. It was their secret."

"My boys never said anything."

"Alex, I doubt they even knew anything about it."

"Daddy," Gracie called out.

"Speak of the . . ." Alex said and bid goodbye to Meredith. She rushed to Gracie's room. "What is it, Gracie?" she asked.

Gracie was sobbing so hard she could hardly catch her breath. "I need my daddy."

Alex didn't want to tell her why her daddy wasn't here; it would terrify Gracie if she knew her grandma Cecile was in the hospital. "Daddy had to go to see a patient at the hospital, but you can tell me why you're crying."

Gracie folded her arms across her chest. "No."

"Well, I love you, but I can't help unless you tell me what happened."

"You love me?" Gracie asked. "I thought you only love Daddy."

"Not only your daddy. I love you very much, and I have a secret for you."

Gracie stopped crying. "What?"

Alex hugged Gracie. "You're really my only little girl, and I need you to do girl things with me."

"When?" Gracie asked.

"Let's leave all the boys and do some girl things this weekend. Wouldn't that be fun?"

Gracie grudgingly agreed.

Alex decided she'd plan a wonderful outing at the mall for just the two of them and leave the boys with David. She put her arm around Gracie. "But first, you have to tell me why you were crying."

"Today, the kids in my class started to say I was the only one who didn't have a mother."

"Gracie, you probably have more people who love you than anyone in your class."

"I told Grandma Cecile, and she told me I could call her Mommy, but she's too old. What if she dies because she's old? Then I'll never find a mommy again."

Alex put her arm around Gracie, and she melted into her. "Don't worry, we're all here for you, and no one's going to die for a long time," Alex said, and she hoped that was true.

CHAPTER 13

As Alex was dressing for work and the March First Friday Book Club meeting, she reached into her closet and pulled out the shoe box she'd found in the attic. The shoe box containing the Christian Louboutin shoes, the ones with the red soles, the ones that cost over two thousand dollars, had been hidden upstairs in the attic inside of a carton labeled BOOKS.

Since David told Alex he'd given away all of Harper's clothes, she was surprised to have found the shoe box and forgot about it until today. She opened the box and looked at the shoes—size seven, Alex's exact size. They were red, bright red. She decided she was going to wear them to the First Friday Book Club meeting. Meredith would certainly be shocked when she saw Alex in those shoes. Terrie would disapprove, and Liz would wonder what had gotten into her best friend.

As she stepped into the right shoe, she felt something, something crammed into the toe. She reached into the shoe and pulled out a little black velvet case tied together with a cord. She opened the velvet case and saw a locket with two hearts. Inside the locket there were two pictures, one on each side, no more than an inch in diameter. One picture was of Harper, but the other picture was of a man, a man who wasn't David.

Alex decided it had to have been a memento from Harper's past, a time before David. But then she turned the locket over and saw an inscription: LOVE FOREVER, NOVEMBER 8, 2012. *Impossible,* she thought. That was six months before Gracie was born.

Confused about the locket, she decided she'd discuss it with her First Friday Book Club women. Surely, they would counsel her about what to do. She was certain showing it to David would destroy him, and there didn't seem to be any reason to tell him about it. But her friends would give her some input. Then again, with Meredith in the book club, she didn't know whether that was wise.

Shocked and uncertain about the locket, she threw it into her attaché case, finished dressing, and rushed out of the bedroom to go downstairs to make the children breakfast. Since David had left earlier than usual to get to the hospital for two caesarian sections, Alex had to get all the children to school: four different schools. Without Cecile, it was difficult to coordinate the children's school and other activities. At least they had arranged for Bethany, their neighbor's daughter, to pick up the children and take them to their after-school activities.

As Alex drove the children to school, she tried to focus her attention on their conversations but kept wondering about the locket, Harper's locket. After the children were successfully dropped off at their various schools, she pulled into her office parking lot and reached for her attaché case. She took out the locket, and for some reason, she peeled back the picture of the man.

There behind the picture of the man was a minuscule photo, a photo of Harper, a pregnant Harper, touching her belly and looking into the lens with an expression that was both provocative and sensual. As Alex stared at the picture, she felt like an intruder—it was so intimate.

Alex's mind went to a dark, suspicious place, and she wondered whether David had any idea that maybe, just maybe, Gracie wasn't his. Alex needed to talk to her First Friday Book Club women, but she feared Meredith would tell Warren, and he'd definitely torment David about it. She looked at her watch: It was already nine thirty and her first patient would be arriving any minute. She had to forget about the locket.

◆◆◆

After treating all of her morning patients, Alex left the office and drove to the March First Friday Book Club meeting. As she rushed to their usual table at the Waters Restaurant, she waved to the women who were already seated and engaged in an animated conversation, most probably not about *The Perfect Nanny,* the March book club selection.

"We ordered for you." Liz motioned for her to take the empty seat next to her.

Practically before sitting down, Alex announced, "There's an issue that I need to discuss with you, but I need to know it will be kept confidential." She looked directly at Meredith. "Especially with you."

"*Moi?*" Meredith pursed her lips. "What did I do? I already offered to leave the book club if you couldn't get over the fact that my husband is not exactly in love with your husband."

"Meredith, I'm over that. This is something that doesn't involve Warren at all."

Liz touched Alex's hand. "You can tell us anything. You know we're here for you." She twirled her strand of pearls. "Nothing has left this room. Ever."

Terrie nodded. "Whatever is said here is as sacred as when my patients confide their deepest fears and secrets to me."

"And you've been psychoanalyzing us for years," Meredith chided.

The waitress delivered their food, Chinese chicken salad all around, even for Terrie, who'd decided to forgo her usual hamburger and fries.

"Where's Judi?" Alex asked.

"Her mother's not doing well," Terrie said. "Again."

"Oh, no." Alex took a sip of water. The group had been together for so long that their cryptic shorthand needed no explanation. They all knew Judi's mother had been ill, terminally ill for so long, and Judi frequently missed the meeting to be at her mother's side.

Meredith took a bite of her salad. "Now, Alex, what's the issue that I'm not to repeat?"

Alex's palms were sweating. "I think David's former wife might have been unfaithful."

"Fidelity is what the couple decides, but the two have to agree," Terrie said, sounding as though she were back in her office, doing couples therapy.

Alex's throat went dry and she could hardly speak. "There's a... a possibility Gracie might not be David's child."

Meredith gasped, Terrie winced, and Liz asked, "Based on what?"

"A scorned lover?" Meredith pursed her lips. "I've had a ton of those."

"Alex, why would you even think Gracie isn't his?" Terrie shook her head. "Makes no sense."

Alex held out the locket. "Look at the date—six months before Gracie was born."

"Oh my God." Meredith put her hand over her mouth. "Gracie loves *moi*, and she's her uncle Warren's world—except for me, that is."

"Let me see that." Liz took the locket, and then passed it to Meredith.

"Corny." Meredith turned it over. "And cheap."

"Not the point." Terrie took it. "Alex, you can't ask David about it."

"Why?" Meredith looked puzzled. "I mean, we're Gracie's auntie and uncle. We deserve to know."

"Meredith, this isn't about you," Alex said softly, promising herself she wasn't going to allow their husbands' issues to invade the First Friday Book Club.

Meredith flipped back a few strands of her long black hair and looked at Alex. "It's always about *moi*. If I don't take care of me, who else will?"

"I thought Warren took such good care of you," Liz said.

"Back to Alex," Terrie said, trying to return their attention to the issue of Gracie's paternity. "Whenever I counsel couples who've had infidelity issues, the main issue is whether they can forgive or not."

"Terrie, even you can't do therapy on a dead wife," Meredith said.

Terrie stabbed at her Chinese chicken salad. "No, but I do know how infidelity destroys marriages."

"Yeah, and so do I—firsthand," Alex said. "My former husband's affair devastated me."

"Telling David would break his heart," Liz said.

"Why even bring it up? He doesn't need to know, and your secret is safe with *moi*." Meredith dramatically put her finger to her lips. "I know I can be caustic at times, but . . ."

"But?" Terrie asked.

"Okay, a little abrasive, but I'm here for you." Meredith pushed her plate away.

Liz laughed. "A little?"

Terrie put down her fork and tugged at the sleeve of her peasant blouse. "But in reality, Harper's dead, and there's no point in twisting a knife in David's heart. The way he worships Gracie . . ."

Liz twirled her long pearl necklace, a sign she was thinking. "Wait a minute, you said *worship*. I think . . ."

"I know where you're going," Alex said. "I thought the same thing. Since Harper was such a devout Catholic, she would never have considered an abortion."

"Right." Liz nodded. "She would have had the child, whether it was David's or not, but . . ."

Terrie took the last bite of her salad. "My advice is it's important to let David hold on to Harper's memory without . . ."

"Does it really matter if he isn't Gracie's natural father?" Liz asked.

"No," Alex said. "David treats Gracie, and all the children for that matter, wonderfully. I don't ever worry about them when he's around."

Meredith held up her copy of this month's selection, *The Perfect Nanny* by Leila Slimani, and sarcastically said, "If you only had the perfect nanny, you wouldn't have to worry about the children at all."

"Meredith, a parent always worries about the children," Terrie said, clearly demonstrating how Meredith's childless life made her unsympathetic to issues of childcare.

"It's our job as parents to keep our children safe in this crazy world," Alex said.

The waitress brought their bill.

Meredith took out her lipstick and started to apply it. "Well, if I had a daughter, I'd never let her out of my sight. And my cats are always in their room whenever we leave."

"I see the parallel," Liz said caustically.

Always eager to point out life lessons and psychological truisms, Terrie said, "Look at what we might have just learned about Harper. I mean, life is like a pinball machine, where the ball takes several turns and then only has one path."

"Clarify," Liz demanded.

Terrie nodded. "At first, we have so many choices: what school to go to, what career path to take, whom to marry, when to have children. . . . Then, as we make those choices, there are fewer and fewer options, but . . ." She stopped and answered her cell phone. "I'm so sorry," she whispered into the phone.

They all knew what the call was. It had been expected—actually, anticipated for six months now. Despite knowing and expecting it, the finality hit them all. They were silent.

Terrie started to cry and the rest of them teared up.

"We all have to be there to support Judi," Liz said.

"Absolutely." Meredith dabbed her eyes. "And if I'm ever going to leave the office in time to get to Judi's, I've got to leave right now."

"I've got to go back and cancel my evening couple," Terrie said. "I hate to do it since they really could benefit from the session, but Judi needs us."

After Meredith and Terrie left, Liz turned to Alex still sitting motionless at the table. "Talk to me. I know we're all upset for Judi, but what are you going to do about the locket?"

"Liz, if this locket and those photos tell a story of Harper's infidelity and David learns Gracie isn't his, he'll be devastated."

Liz put her arm around Alex. "You can't tell him."

CHAPTER 14

Since Alex wanted to join the First Friday Book Club women at Judi's house to support her, she called David. He told her she didn't have to rush home; he could handle the children. He said he'd be able to get home in time to relieve Bethany.

Alex had some trepidation about Bethany after Eric told her during breakfast that he'd been late to his game two days ago because Bethany had stopped at a friend's house to pick up some schoolwork. And, Eric complained, she stayed at her friend's house for fifteen minutes and left him in the car with Gracie and Jon. Alex decided she'd have a talk with Bethany, but right now, she needed her.

Alex thought maybe, just maybe, Eric might have been overly critical since he was so very upset about his father. His father, Gabe, had called last night and told him he'd been sentenced and was going to be sent to prison for five years for the Medicare fraud. On top of that, Gabe told Eric there was a large fine; therefore, he wouldn't be able to contribute to Eric's college education. Alex also knew there was the even more challenging court case coming. Gabe would soon go on trial for his part in the murder-for-hire plan he'd initiated against Alex during their contentious child custody case.

In fact, last night, after Eric had gotten off the phone with Gabe, he turned to Alex and broke down. He sobbed, and she held him. Then, to her shock and gratitude, he apologized for all the horrible things he'd said to her about being the cause of his father's impending prison sentence.

Just last month, Eric had accused Alex of making up lies to hurt Gabe, accusations he'd probably heard from Gabe. He'd been overly defensive of his father when Alex tried to tell him her side. But after Gabe had confessed his guilt to Eric, Gabe also had begged him never to be as greedy as he'd been. After the phone call, Eric had virtually turned around. His previously unwavering loyalty to his father had been compromised.

The relationship with Eric was definitely getting better, and Alex wanted to savor that. Yes, she knew how strong the bond between a parent and child was, especially now as she drove to join her First Friday Book Club women at Judi's house.

To Alex's surprise, Judi seemed to be coping well. Maybe, Alex thought, it was because her relationship with her mother had been so strong, supportive, and there was a modicum of peace; something Alex never had either during her mother's life or upon her death.

After helping Judi and her husband with the funeral arrangements, the women went into the family room. Judi told them stories about her mother—loving, caring stories. It was like a warm coat that Alex wanted to borrow and slip into, to feel a mother's warmth. It was then she decided she was going to be that to her children. When it was her time, she wanted the children to think of her with this much admiration and love.

They talked until almost midnight.

◆◆◆

When Alex entered the house and saw David sitting in his favorite chair, listening to music, and reading *Before We Were Yours,* she kissed his cheek.

David took off his headset and asked how Judi was doing.

"As well as can be expected. Her mother was her rock."

He nodded. "At least she had her mother for this long, and . . ."

"I know," she said. Yes, Alex knew how much he worried about Gracie, and how difficult these past two years since her mother's death had been for her. And as wonderful a father as David was, she knew he couldn't compensate for a mother's love. For a daughter, the absence of that relationship leaves a void—that Alex knew firsthand.

He pointed to the novel on his lap. "This should be your book club selection. It's about an orphanage where children were kept, and . . ."

"We do need an uplifting book for a change," she said.

"This isn't." He shook his head. "The children were stolen and then sold. A parent has to be so vigilant; one careless second and the child's gone. In this book, when the father took the mother to the hospital to give birth, they left their children on the houseboat. That night the children were taken by some predator and placed in an orphanage which was really a prison."

"I don't understand," she said. "Why were they taken to an orphanage?"

"Wealthy people who couldn't have children would buy the children from the orphanage. The supposedly caring owner of the orphanage would tell the prospective parents the children were abandoned by their parents or their parents were dead."

"Where was that?" she asked.

"It's based a real orphanage in Memphis, Tennessee, in the 1930s, but something like that could happen, even today. That's why I was always telling Cecile, and now Bethany, to be careful, lock all the doors, and never leave Gracie alone even for a second, especially when she drives someplace with her."

She knew how worried, vigilant, he was, but a parent had to be; that was today's sad reality.

Then he put his book on the little table. "And, Alex, we're getting an au pair."

"Why the sudden change of heart?" she asked, pleased he'd finally agreed with her. She'd been lobbying for an au pair for a month now, but he'd refused to consider it, claiming Cecile would be able to watch Gracie once her insulin level was under control.

He pointed to the coffee table. "Look at this."

Alex glanced down at the table, which was strewn with puzzle pieces and crayons. When she'd come into the house, she did notice the kitchen was in total disarray.

"Alex, there were dirty glasses and plates on the table. Ants were crawling all over the kitchen, but . . ."

Her chest tightened. "But?"

"When I pulled up, Bethany was outside smoking and talking on her cell."

"Where were the kids?"

He took a deep breath. "Gracie was in the bathtub."

"David, I would have fired her on the spot."

"We have to do it tactfully."

"Tactfully?" she asked, terrified about what could have happened. They had to be more careful. It was their job, every parent's job, to protect their children.

"Bethany's parents were my closest friends."

"Gracie was in the bathtub," she repeated, unable to comprehend his reluctance about firing her. "We're not friends. You and

Harper were their friends, but they've never even said hello to me. They act like I moved right in, took advantage of a situation . . ."

"Why don't you take advantage of me now." He put his arms around her.

Alex hugged him, a hug that was filled with relief, relief that nothing had happened to Gracie, and, she was determined, nothing would.

CHAPTER 15

Alex and David decided they'd spend the weekend searching for an au pair. But first, Saturday was pancake day, so everyone assembled at the kitchen table, ready to wolf down breakfast and then get on with their activities. Eric was going to hang out with his friends and play basketball. Daniel planned to work on his science project, but Jon said he had nothing to do.

"Me too," Gracie said, evolving more and more into Jon's ally.

"I have lots of chores for children who have nothing to do," Alex said. She wanted them to be appreciative of each and every privilege they had and refused to tolerate laziness.

Jon furrowed his brows. "I just thought of something I could do."

"Me too," Gracie repeated and then looked at Jon. "What are we doing?"

David laughed. Then he leaned across the kitchen table and whispered something to Gracie.

Jon shook his head. "It's not nice to tell secrets."

Gracie blurted out, "My daddy said he needs help with some more planting, and whoever helps gets to go in the pool later."

Daniel took his plate to the sink. "I have to finish my project by tonight, so I can't plant."

"Daniel, do we need to get anything at the hardware store for your project?" Alex asked.

"Thanks, Mom, but I've got it under control." Daniel started to walk up the stairs.

Eric helped himself to another pancake.

Gracie turned to Jon. "What should we do now?"

"I'm doing the planting with your dad," Jon said.

"Daddy, why aren't there girl things to do?"

Alex looked at her watch. "I've got an idea. Why don't Gracie and I go to the mall?"

Gracie appeared panic-stricken. "I don't leave my daddy on the weekend . . . unless Grandma Cecile takes me someplace."

David put down his fork. "Yes, I think it would be lovely for the girls to go to the mall."

"You can come with us," Gracie offered.

David winked at Alex. "Maybe some little girl needs a dress for Easter."

"And for Passover," Alex said.

"Of course," David said. "Passover."

"David, remember you agreed we could do both." Alex wanted to keep tradition for her boys, and although David was Jewish, he'd told her he'd promised Harper they would raise Gracie as a Catholic. And he'd told her, after Harper's death, he was even more committed to making sure Gracie followed her mother's religion.

Jon smiled. "Passover is my best holiday because of all the money I get."

"Money?" Gracie asked. "Kids get money?"

Alex smiled at Gracie. "Yes, the adults buy the matzoh from the kids if they can't find where the kids had hidden it."

Gracie ran to the pantry, opened the door, and started to look over the shelves. Then she returned to the kitchen table, a box of matzoh in her hand. "How much for this?"

Alex took the box. "Let me explain. The youngest child—"

"That's me!" Gracie screamed. "Jon, how much money do I get?"

"No," Alex said. "It's part of a tradition during the Passover dinner. The children steal the matzoh and—"

Gracie shook her head. "You guys just told me you get money for finding it. Now you're saying I have to steal it."

"It's a Jewish tradition," Alex said. Since she'd been observant for so many years, she'd forgotten how the myriad of rules and traditions could appear confusing to a child who wasn't familiar. Just as she was starting to explain to Gracie, Jon stepped in.

Jon put an arm around Gracie. "It's true. My brothers and I steal the matzoh and then hide it, but the Seder can't continue until the adults find it."

"What's a Seder?" Gracie looked even more confused than before.

"We'll have a fabulous Seder this year," Alex said. "It's right after Easter, so it's the perfect time for all of us to celebrate both."

Obviously no longer interested in Passover, once it was established that she wouldn't get money until there was a ceremony, Gracie crawled onto David's lap. "Did you forget about the dress for Easter?"

David kissed her cheek. "You go to the mall with Alex. I've got to stay here and plant." He looked at Alex. "Then I'm going to start the au pair process."

"I need to decide on the au pair too," Alex said, wondering if they would ask the right questions and wondering what the right questions were for the person to whom you were about to entrust your children's safety.

Eric grabbed yet another pancake. "Do I have to give up my room?"

"Of course not," Alex said. "She'll have Cecile's room."

Gracie started to cry. "No one's taking Grandma's room."

"Right, Gracie," David said. "I don't want to upset Cecile. We have another option."

They all looked at him, waiting, wondering.

"The downstairs sitting room," he said, and pointed to the room off the front entry. The plush white suede couch and two red and black wing chairs, separated by a coffee table with a black granite top, had never been used, not since Alex had moved in and probably even before that. The only useful part of the room was the floor-to-ceiling bookcase that housed an alphabetically arranged collection of novels, which Alex had promised herself she'd start to read once she had more time.

"What about a closet?" Alex asked.

"It's behind the bookshelves," David said.

"Cool," Eric said. "A hidden closet." He got up and went to the room.

They all followed him.

Eric called up to Daniel. "Get down here and see this."

"What else is there hidden in this house?" Alex asked, and as soon as she said it, she was sorry. Yes, every house had secrets; that she knew all too well.

Secrets pulled her back, back to the day her father had invited her downstairs to the basement to see a surprise—the day that changed her life. She'd followed him along the narrow hallway to a closet. There in the closet was a carton. Her father had dug through several books that were in the carton to get to a jewelry box with porcelain fruit on top. He'd given the jewelry box to Alex, explaining it belonged to his sister, who'd died before Alex was born, and he knew she would have wanted Alex to have it.

Appreciatively, Alex had accepted the jewelry box and then turned her attention to the books inside the carton. She'd picked up *The Fountainhead* by Ayn Rand and asked her father if she could have it.

"Sure," he'd said, and sealed the box as she started upstairs with the book. She'd closed her bedroom door and read *The Fountainhead*—until she turned to page fifty. A picture had fallen onto the floor. She'd grabbed it. In the picture, her father and a man she didn't recognize were looking at each other, looking straight into each other's eyes—like they were in love.

She'd turned the picture over and read the inscription, "Love forever," and her world changed from predictable to one charged with secrets. Then, she understood why her father believed her mother when she'd explained the burn on Alex's wrist was an accident. Yes, it was then that Alex realized her mother kept her father's secret because he kept hers.

Eric plopped down on the couch. "Can this be my room?"

"You have the best room of all," Alex said, reminding him of how lucky he was to finally have his own room. It was important to her that the children were appreciative of all they had.

David closed the door. "This room will be perfect, and there's sufficient privacy 'cause the door is double-paned."

"But what about a shower?" Alex asked.

"She can shower in the pool house. The bathroom there is very private," David said, and walked back to the kitchen to wash the breakfast dishes.

Gracie followed. "Daddy, when will Grandma be able to watch me again?" The excitement of the hidden closet was obviously not impressing her.

"We better get ready, Gracie. We're going to the mall!" Alex said.

"Me too," Jon said.

"Girls only. You don't want to be looking at dresses."

David put his arm around Jon. "We can turn on the heater for the pool."

Jon smiled. "Mommy, you can go to the mall without me."

CHAPTER 16

On the drive to the mall, Alex asked questions, mostly about Gracie's kindergarten and the upcoming Easter pageant at her school. Gracie started to relax more and even got excited about doing a girl thing together.

When they got to the South Coast Plaza mall and passed the carousel, Gracie stopped. "Can I go on the ride?"

"You can go for a ride as soon as we find a dress for you." Alex took her hand.

Then Gracie pointed to the sign with the picture of an Easter Bunny. "Can I come and see the Easter Bunny?"

"Sure," Alex promised. "Now, what color dress do you think the Easter Bunny loves?"

"Pink," Gracie said. "And that's Grandma Cecile and Uncle Warren's favorite color. Both of them."

"Well then, pink it is." Alex knew how much Gracie adored her uncle and wished it was easier between him and David. But David continued to balk at attending functions where he'd be forced to interact with Warren. In fact, Alex was sure he wouldn't have even gone to Warren and Meredith's wedding if Gracie hadn't been the flower girl. That would have been a shame, because if that had happened, Alex and David would never have reconnected. Interesting how some coincidences become the turning points in our lives.

Gracie looked up at her. "Will my daddy take me to see the Easter Bunny?"

"I'm sure he will," Alex said. Since Cecile had become ill, Gracie seemed to be even more dependent on David. And Alex was sure Gracie probably feared that Cecile, too, would die. After losing her mother, any child would feel a heightened fear about the fragility of life, and Alex decided she was going to do whatever she could to make life safe, predictable for Gracie.

Once they got to the Nordstrom girls' department, they went directly to the 6X dresses. Alex would hold up one dress after another, and Gracie would shake her head and say, "No thank you, but thank you for asking," her favorite expression. Then, Gracie saw the dress: pink ruffles covering the entire skirt and a pink top with little pink roses. It looked like every girl's dream.

Alex helped Gracie try it on.

The saleswoman peeked into the room. "Wow, you're so beautiful."

"Yes," Alex agreed. "Beautiful, ballerina beautiful."

Gracie smiled as she looked in the mirror. "I love it."

Alex paid for the dress. "Let's have some lunch."

They went to the café in Nordstrom, where they shared a turkey sandwich and chatted about Gracie's upcoming ballet lessons and how much her daddy wanted her to play soccer. But Gracie was adamant: soccer wasn't for girls. They giggled about boys and men loving sports more than things—girl things—like ballet. This was even more fun than Alex had anticipated.

Suddenly, Gracie missed her father and wanted to go home to him. She even decided to forgo the carousel ride but insisted she wanted to return to see the Easter parade.

When they got home, everyone was in the family room, talking animatedly.

"David, you really were busy on the au pair site," she teased.

David smirked. "Application is printed on the table for us to do tonight."

Eric was positively bursting with excitement. "Mom, David has to tell you the best part."

Alex put her hands on her hips. "I'm almost afraid to ask."

"Um." David looked at Eric. "Should we tell her?"

Alex was thrilled with the bonding that seemed to have occurred today, but she was cautious, her usual caution always nagging at her. She decided to fall into the embrace of her new family and enjoy. "Okay, what else?"

David said, "The au pair will—"

"The au pair we don't have yet?" Alex shook her head.

"As I was saying before someone interrupted me"—David put his arm around her—"the au pair will need a car, so . . ."

Alex looked at Eric, who was beaming, and waited.

David winked at Eric. "Well, Eric and I were looking at cars because, as I said, the au pair will need a car, and so will Eric when he turns sixteen, and . . ."

She laughed, a delighted, appreciative laugh. "You really have been scheming. Thank goodness I never left you alone before."

"We found such a neat Accord," Eric said. "It's only three years old, and wow . . ."

"This is going to be trouble." Alex leaned over David's shoulder and looked at the picture of an Accord. She rubbed his back. She knew even if David had promised to buy Eric a car earlier in their relationship, that wouldn't have turned Eric around. It was his father's sentencing and confession to Eric that made him forgive Alex and finally realize she wasn't the one who'd caused the disintegration of their family; it was Gabe who'd left and then committed one criminal act after another.

"Well?" Eric looked at her, knowing he needed her approval.

"You'll have to get good grades," she said.

"Easy," Eric said. "Like I've told you before, Daniel isn't the only brain around here."

Alex looked approvingly at the car. "And a job to pay for gas."

Eric and David shared a nod.

"Mr. Barnett at the gas station already told me I could cashier there when I'm sixteen," Eric said.

"Wow," Alex said, surprised. "You really accomplished a lot, but aren't gas stations dangerous? I mean, there have been shootings in gas stations."

Daniel turned to his cell phone and brought up a picture of a recent gas station shooting. "Just last week."

Alex looked at Daniel's phone. "What about a job at the mall?"

Eric scowled. "You think the mall is safe?"

◆◆◆

After dinner, David turned on the laptop and pulled up the Au Pair in the United States website. He'd already created the family ID and had read all about the program. He and Alex scrolled down and looked at about a hundred photos of women, almost all pictured with a smiling child or children looking adoringly at them.

He reviewed the financial commitment: There was a fee for matching and a program fee, and then they were required to pay a weekly stipend of about two hundred dollars. However, the au pairs were only allowed to work forty hours a week, which would be fine, except for holidays.

David pointed at the computer screen. "Who should we ask to fill out the Host Family Confidential Personal Reference form?"

"Liz, of course," Alex said.

"This asks for the personal reference person's view of the family and the number of times the person has visited us," David read. "What do you think Liz will say about our family?"

"We're crazy," Alex teased and then studied the screen. "'Abnormal conditions?' Liz will have lots to say about that."

"Okay, let's go to the family part," David said, and then called to the children. "Kids, we need you to come down to answer questions."

"Am I in trouble?" Gracie called back from her room.

David smiled. "No, it's a form we have to fill out about our whole family."

Jon and Gracie came downstairs.

Gracie sat down in her little red sling-back chair right next to Jon's blue chair in the family room. "Are we the whole family?" she asked.

"No," Alex said, and called the older boys since they hadn't responded when David summoned them.

Daniel and Eric came into the room.

David read, "Are you currently expecting?"

"You called us down for this?" Daniel asked. Usually cooperative, this was uncharacteristic of him, but he'd probably been engrossed in his school project.

Eric laughed. "I'd like to know if there's going to be another kid!"

Alex reached over and turned Eric's baseball cap around, visor forward. He was now taller than she. He was even developing a sense of humor. At almost sixteen, he was surprisingly becoming gentler and more cooperative toward everyone in the house.

Eric returned his hat to the backwards position he loved. "Mom, it's *in* to wear it this way."

She nodded to David. "Let's go to the rest of the questions about the family."

Gracie looked around the room. "Daddy, are we a family now?"

"Yes," he said, and read the computer screen. "Are we planning to adopt a child under the age of two?"

Gracie's eyes widened. "Are we getting more children? And can I have a sister instead of another boy?"

Eric tousled her hair. "Gracie, don't you like us anymore?"

David read, "Now, what are our general interests?"

Daniel walked over and pointed to the computer. "Here are the choices. Everyone pick one: writing, arts and crafts, dance . . ."

"Give me a break," Eric said, returning to his usual teenage annoyance with anything that didn't pertain to sports. "I'm out of here."

Alex looked at him sternly.

"Put down arts and crafts for me." Eric shook his head.

David typed and then looked up. "Actually, Eric, this part is for you. It asks about athletics."

Jon furrowed his brow. "Aren't I a good athlete?"

"Of course," Alex said. "But they want to know specific sports."

"Is ballerina sports?" Gracie asked, wide-eyed.

"No, Gracie, it's dancing." David swooped her up from her chair and started to twirl around, holding her in his arms. "What a fabulous dancer."

"Daddy, you did it all."

"Gracie girl, you are a great dance partner, so we can put that down for you," David said.

Gracie shook her head. "But it has to be sports."

Daniel, usually protective of Jon, stepped in to show kindness to Gracie. "Dancing could be a sport. Look at figure skating."

"I don't want to do skating." Gracie started to pirouette. "I want to be a ballerina or an athlete person like all of you."

David returned his attention to the screen. "Next section. Are we religious?"

Gracie put her hands on her hips and smugly replied. "Yes, Grandma Cecile and I go to religion all the time at the big church."

Daniel plopped down on the couch. "I'm definitely religious. Remember, my Bar Mitzvah was last summer."

Gracie tugged at David's sleeve. "Daddy, can I have a party at church like Daniel did?"

"I'm going to have one, and you get money." Jon smirked.

David shook his head. "Gracie, your mother wanted you to be raised Catholic, so you can't have a Bat Mitzvah."

"Daddy, I didn't say that Bat Missa word. I said I want a party like Daniel."

Alex knew how much Gracie loved parties and didn't want her to be resentful of anything having to do with the boys. She said, "Wait until you see how hard Jon will have to work for his Bar Mitzvah, and—"

"Well." Gracie shrugged her shoulders. "I can be Jewish too."

"Usually, a person is just one religion," Alex said, and then looked at David. He was scowling, and she feared she shouldn't have said that. He might have thought she was undermining him, testing his allegiance to his promise to raise Gracie as a Catholic.

"Being Catholic is good," she said to Gracie. Then she was certain; Harper's religious belief was definitely the reason she wouldn't have had an abortion even if the child wasn't David's.

"Okay." David pointed to the screen. "What did we decide? Are we religious?"

Gracie shook her head so hard her big bow fell to the floor. "Daddy, you're not religion 'cause you never go to church with Grandma Cecile and me."

"Gracie, I don't go because I'm Jewish."

Gracie pointed to the boys. "Like them?"

CHAPTER 17

F inally, after several days of looking through the au pair site, they made a preliminary decision: Sonia, a twenty-year-old Colombian student, was their first choice. Although her experience caring for children had been limited to her five siblings, her availability was immediate, which suited them perfectly. And her eagerness to come to the United States was obvious.

"She's almost too good to be true," David said.

"Alarm," Alex said. "I told you about *The Perfect Nanny*. I'm a little skeptical."

"Can you stop with your book club?" David teased.

Alex called Gracie to her. "Today we have to have an interview," she said. "Do you know what that means?"

"Yes, you have to talk here instead of doing fun stuff."

David hoisted Gracie onto his lap. "We have to find someone who'll be a good babysitter for you."

"Only Grandma Cecile would be fun," Gracie protested. "Why can't I stay with Grandma?"

David kissed Gracie on the head. "She can't come and take care of you because she's a little sick, and she can't drive or—"

"Daddy, what if she dies?"

"She's not going to die," he reassured her. "But it's too hard for her to drive."

Alex knew he was worried. Gracie would be devastated if anything happened to her grandma. In a sense, Cecile had assumed the role of mother for the past few years during Harper's illness and after her death.

Gracie put her hands on her hips. "So, why can't I go to her house?"

Alex looked empathetically at Gracie. "Sometimes, she falls asleep and then there would be no one to watch you." Alex didn't say they also needed someone who could drive and take the boys to their activities and then watch Jon. She wouldn't say that; that could make Gracie resent Jon. And Alex and Gracie were growing closer, and she didn't want to do anything to diminish that. Gracie was even starting to spend more time in the kitchen instead of going to her room. Their relationship was starting to feel natural, good.

"I could go to the hospital with you, Daddy."

"Gracie girl, you can't. They don't allow children in the operating room. Let's see how nice Sonia is." He dialed up the Skype connection.

"Hello, Gracie." Sonia waved, but she looked down, avoiding eye contact.

Reluctantly, Gracie looked at the screen. "Hi."

"Liking to play with dolls?" Sonia held up a doll. "This one, my best, I bring it to you one day?"

"Okay," Gracie said, and then ran to her room while Alex and David continued talking.

Gracie returned with her stuffed animal. "This is my Chicken Love. See the mommy and the baby?" She held up her bright yellow chicken.

113

"Yes," Sonia said, but she didn't seem to understand what Gracie was saying about her Chicken Love.

Gracie kissed her Chicken Love. "My mommy gave it to me, but this baby gets to stay with the mommy forever, and the mommy doesn't die."

David pulled her close.

The older boys dutifully waved at the screen, obviously uninterested in someone who was going to move into the house and be "a part of the family."

Then Alex and David asked her the rest of the questions they'd carefully scripted, but Alex wondered how beneficial an interview could be. She recalled the interview of the nanny in *The Perfect Nanny*. If only the parents in the novel had asked the nanny the right questions, maybe the children would have been safe. If only . . . She thought how many times she'd said to herself, *If only*.

She had to erase that from her mind, but the diabolical things people did to children were ubiquitous. On any given day, the news was filled with one sensational story after another about horrible things like child abuse or abduction . . . or worse.

David motioned to Alex.

"Could we please see your room?" Alex asked. They'd decided it was more appropriate for Alex to ask the question about viewing Sonia's room. They'd also decided her room would be a good indication of how neat she was, whether there was anything amiss. After reading *The Perfect Nanny*, Alex had told David about the importance of checking out as much as possible. And she'd recounted how, in the book, the nanny's home was an indication of her eccentricities.

"Room?" Sonia asked, and then nodded. Her room was meticulous—everything perfectly arranged and nothing of any questionable nature.

Then Alex asked why she wanted to come to America.

Hesitating and groping for the right words, Sonia explained she'd had a fall and fractured her hip. Since she was distraught about the fact that her career as a ballerina, a dream she'd had since she was five years old, was destroyed, she had decided to become an au pair.

Upon hearing the word *ballerina*, Gracie jumped up out of her seat and said, "I'm going to be a ballerina too." Then Gracie demonstrated the first three positions she'd just learned in ballet class.

As though suddenly on familiar ground, in her milieu, Sonia changed from shy and retiring to excited, animated. She got up from her chair and showed Gracie how to maintain all of the positions properly. Then she did a few twirls and steps, probably from her former routine.

Gracie couldn't take her eyes off Sonia. She was mesmerized by the display—a real ballerina, dancing right in front of her. After Sonia finished, Gracie was captivated and crawled onto David's lap. "Can she be my babysitter?" Gracie asked.

"Yes?" David looked at Alex.

Alex wasn't completely convinced. Sonia's English was rudimentary, and she had difficulty holding a conversation. However, once she was engaged in ballet, she came alive. In ballet, there was no language barrier. Although Sonia's lack of self-confidence unnerved Alex, there was something charming about her. And Alex hoped she could be trusted in an emergency.

After much deliberation, Alex and David decided they were a good fit. Within the next twenty-four hours, they'd each put a hold on their applications, which meant they were not going to look for any other matches. The au pair company would then begin to process Sonia's paperwork. Since Sonia already had her passport, work visa, and even had an international driver's license, the actual date of employment would be dependent upon how fast the paperwork could be completed.

They signed off and started to fill out the request to place a hold.

"She's not such a looker," Eric said.

Alex turned to Eric, beseeching him not to say anything negative in front of Gracie, especially when Gracie had told David she thought Sonia was pretty. Actually, Alex thought Sonia was attractive, but she was glad Eric didn't concur. She wouldn't have to worry about having a young woman in the house with an adolescent male.

"Okay," Eric said. "She seems nice."

"Yes." Daniel agreed, less than enthusiastically.

Alex looked at her older sons, appreciative of their neutral comments in front of the little ones. She needed their support in convincing Gracie everything would be fine. And she needed Jon to be comfortable with Sonia as soon as possible.

The boys went back upstairs, and Gracie cuddled into David until he announced, "I'm taking you upstairs. Time for bed."

As David got up and carried Gracie, she asked, "How many stories?"

Her father looked at her with mock seriousness. "Were you good today?"

"Daddy, I'm always good."

Alex smiled: a girl and her daddy. She wished she could capture this moment forever. David was a wonderful father. At times like this, touching, sweet moments, Alex missed her own father. Dead for five years. Even after she'd learned his darkest secret, he was still her hero. She also knew it was right to have kept her suspicion about the locket to herself.

CHAPTER 18

After two weeks of trying to coordinate babysitters and rides for the boys' sports, Alex and David were relieved Sonia was scheduled to arrive this afternoon at three. They decided it would be best if Alex went alone to pick her up at LAX. It would give Sonia a little time to acclimate before meeting the entire family.

Alex woke with a start. When she realized it was only eight o'clock and the children weren't downstairs yet, she cuddled into David. He was her dream come true, kind and loving.

He leaned over and kissed her cheek. "Before pancakes for the kids, I have a treat for us."

As he stroked her back, Alex melted into his gentle touch.

She turned to him and wrapped her leg across his thighs, their sign. He knew she wanted him.

They kissed.

"The door," she whispered.

He got up and closed the door. As he walked back to bed, he stopped and threw his pajama bottoms onto the floor.

Just looking at him made her tingle. She eagerly took off her nightgown.

He got into bed and kissed her lips. Then he took her nipple in his mouth, and she reached down and stroked his already erect penis.

He started to suck her nipple, first gently, then more fervently, hungrily. He moved his hand down her body and spread her legs apart. He stroked her and then softly inserted his finger into her vagina.

"David," she moaned.

"I want you," he said, voice gravelly, urgent.

She climbed on top of him.

They looked at each other, excited for the pleasure they knew they'd give.

He kissed her and rolled her over onto her back. As though engaged in a perfectly choreographed dance, he mounted her.

Ready for him, she felt herself moisten.

He slid his penis into her, and they moved together slowly, then with an urgency, as though they were magnets for each other, unable to stop until they came.

"Oh my God," he whispered as he came.

Feeling him to her core, she shuddered. There was no other place in the world she wanted to be at this moment than with David, her husband, her lover.

He rolled off of her, and they smiled at each other, a satisfied secret smile.

"Pancakes." She started to get up.

"I'm afterglowing," he said.

She laughed and went to put on her robe. "The kids are probably waiting for breakfast."

"Be down in a few," he promised.

Breakfast was a strategy session. Since Sonia was arriving later in the day, they needed to go over all the details: Sonia's room had to be readied. The children were told they had to be welcoming to Sonia. There were rules for how they were to act toward her and, most importantly, how they had to continue to do their chores.

Then they started to prepare Sonia's room. David and the older boys took the couch and two chairs that were in the sitting room upstairs to make room for the bed. Then they brought down one of the two beds from Cecile's room, the room no one was to use—except Cecile.

Even though they'd discussed it and planned how they were going to move each piece of furniture, Gracie started to cry when she saw them bring down one of the beds from Cecile's room. Gracie clutched her Chicken Love to her chest. "You have to leave the two beds in my grandma's room 'cause sometimes I have to sleep with her there."

David looked at her. "We talked about how it was only temporary. Do you know what temporary is?"

"Grandma Cecile could stay with me all the time. Not temporary."

David swooped her up and gave her a hug. "I have an idea. We can buy a special little bed and put it in Grandma Cecile's room so you can sleep there when she comes over."

Alex looked at him, wondering why he was promising something that could never come to fruition. Cecile's health had been declining almost every day since she was released from the hospital. Although David thought it best to tell Cecile the truth, Warren had the power as her son to decide what she was to be told. And Warren was adamant: she was not to be told she had Alzheimer's.

"Do you need me anymore?" Daniel asked. "I'm sweaty from the lifting and going to shower."

"Me too," Jon mimicked, although he hadn't done any lifting. Daniel and Jon went upstairs.

"Any more pancakes?" Eric walked back to the kitchen.

"Daddy," Gracie said. "I have a better idea. I want you to put Grandma Cecile's other bed in my room for when she comes."

Then she put her hands on her hips. "But then what about my tea set?"

"We can move your tea set and table," David said.

"I need my tea set. How can we do the tea party?"

"We could have tea on the big table," Alex offered. "With real teacups. And maybe Sonia wants to come to a tea party."

"Is Sonia going to be part of our family?" Gracie asked.

David patted Gracie on the head, her long brown hair glistening under the light. "We have to treat her like she's part of our family."

Gracie kissed her bright yellow Chicken Love. "Sonia likes Chicken Love, too, but how many people are we going to let into the family now?"

"Gracie, let's go up and get dressed," David said.

Gracie started to go upstairs and then stopped. "Wait, does Sonia have to watch me today?"

"No," David said. "She doesn't start until Monday."

Gracie grabbed his leg. "So, you'll stay with me all day?"

David picked Gracie up to carry her upstairs. "Today, I have to take Sonia out for a little while to make sure she's a good driver before . . ."

"Isn't it a little too late for that?" Eric asked. "And with my car."

"Eric," Alex cautioned. "Gratitude and humility or there won't be any car."

Eric looked at David. "I'm sorry. I really appreciate the car."

Before Alex left for the airport, she reminded the boys they'd have to be very welcoming and respectful to Sonia, especially today, her first day with the family.

As they'd arranged, Alex parked the car and then walked to the international arrivals sign at LAX and waited. Within twenty-five minutes, Sonia arrived looking a little tired but excited. On the long car ride home from the airport, Alex wondered if hiring Sonia was the right choice. Her shyness was a little unnerving. But she thought about Sonia's good qualities and decided she was being too critical. It would all work out.

◆◆◆

Sonia's first two weeks were uneventful. As a matter of fact, they were perfect, too perfect. Sonia got the children off to school without a problem, picked them up on time, and seemed to fit into the family wonderfully. Sonia and Gracie worked on ballet steps, and Sonia even choreographed a performance, which Gracie gave to the family. Gracie was smitten; therefore, so was David.

But Daniel, usually the warmest and most welcoming, seemed cautious, almost hesitant, to engage Sonia. Jon occasionally complained about the fact that now Gracie was too busy with ballet and wouldn't play games with him. Eric and Sonia immediately formed a friendship, which included English lessons designed to elevate Sonia's very rudimentary knowledge of English.

Although Sonia seemed to be a little more at ease with the family, she was reluctant to dine with them even when offered. But to Alex's surprise, Sonia had made a friend at the park and had almost daily outings with this friend. She'd told Alex the lady was taking care of a baby boy and lived somewhere around the corner. Sonia didn't know exactly where her new friend worked, but she knew it was within walking distance of the park.

It was all working out.

Today, the Saturday before Easter, Alex had offered Sonia the day off, but she declined, stating she'd rather stay with Gracie and take her to the South Coast Plaza shopping mall to see the Easter Bunny.

They all had breakfast, and then in her best English, Sonia told Gracie, "We go upstairs for Easter Bunny dress. Bunny telled me he give chocolate for girls who dress pink."

Gracie put her hands on her hips and turned to Alex. "Is that true?"

"I don't know," Alex said. "You always look beautiful, and I know the Easter Bunny will think so too."

"Can I go?" Eric asked.

Daniel laughed. "Aren't you over the Easter Bunny?"

"I need sneakers, so I want to go."

"Eric, isn't it easier to go online?" Alex asked.

"Sure, but I want to try them on in the mall and then order online."

Alex agreed. "Sonia, we'll join you."

"Can Jon come with us?" Gracie asked.

Although Gracie was in awe of Sonia's ballet prowess, on rare occasions she didn't seem entirely comfortable with Sonia and wanted Jon to accompany them. This made Alex anxious, fearing maybe Gracie had some sixth sense. Or, Alex reassured herself, Gracie really enjoyed Jon's company.

"Sonia," Alex said. "We're all going, but I need fifteen minutes to finish some calls."

Sonia looked uncomfortable. "I need leave now."

There was something that wasn't right with her reaction—some urgency, a need to leave right away. Maybe, Alex thought, Sonia was meeting that friend. Something!

"Oh, I have to change my shoes," Sonia said, grabbed her cell phone, and went to her room.

Alex watched her hurry out of the room and wondered why she seemed so agitated. Maybe something was bothering her. Alex decided she would ask Sonia tonight.

When Sonia returned, she looked at Gracie. "You wear Easter dress?"

"No thank you. That's my dress for Easter when Grandma Cecile and Uncle Warren come to the party at our house," Gracie said. She always picked out her own outfits. Cecile had gotten her into that habit. Gracie enjoyed being able to make her own decisions. It gave her some power over something in her world, giving her independence where it didn't really affect anything else. Today, she'd picked the white dress with the little flowers, her garden dress, as she called it.

"Daniel, are you sure you don't want to come to the mall?" Alex called up to him.

Daniel walked into the kitchen. "Some kids are going to see Henning Morales' film, *The Dirt Merchants,* and ...."

Jon looked at him quizzically. "You're going to a movie about dirt?"

Daniel smiled at Jon. "No, it's supposed to be motivational—get you excited about doing the right thing."

Gracie shook her head. "Wouldn't you rather get chocolate from the Easter Bunny."

"Remember, I just had my Bar Mitzvah, so the Easter Bunny won't give me chocolate."

"He's a good bunny." Gracie laughed. "Just like my Chicken Love."

Daniel tapped Gracie on the head. "Then bring me some chocolate from the bunny."

"You believe in the Easter Bunny?" Jon asked his brother.

Sonia appeared to be getting impatient, eager to leave.

As Lucky nuzzled Alex, she bent down and petted the dog. "Daniel, as long as you're not going, please walk her."

"I usually run her," Eric said smugly.

Alex lifted Lucky's face to her and said, "You don't care whether you walk or run, do you, Lucky?" Funny how different the boys were. Eric was the consummate jock while Daniel was the scholar, and Jon was a mixture. Eric was more like his father, Gabe—everything was easy for him. Gabe had sailed through medical school and taken to track easily—everything was easy. He got whatever he wanted. Maybe he'd even taken the money from his partners because it was easy. Then it had escalated, and he'd billed Medicare for a patient he hadn't examined, just one patient. He'd gotten paid, and his Medicare billing fraud had escalated. He'd billed for a few more patients and then more. It'd started easy, but in reality, at first, he was just lucky. Lucky—funny that's what the boys had named their dog.

Gabe was no longer lucky. Maybe, she thought, luck worked until you challenged it, took it for granted.

They got into the car, and Eric sat in the front.

Sonia started to put Gracie in her car seat. "I sit in back with childrens."

"It's children, not childrens," Eric corrected.

"Thank you, Eric," Sonia said.

Alex noted Sonia's English had actually improved a little in only two weeks, probably because she and Eric practiced together almost every day. Aside from Gracie, he was the one with whom she seemed the most relaxed. Maybe it was his own awkwardness as a teenager and she barely an adult.

Eric turned around.

In the rearview mirror, Alex saw Sonia smile at Eric and then she thought she saw her wink. She'd have to talk to him tonight. Hormones could make him do things; she'd have to remind him of that. She couldn't talk to Sonia; that would be accusatory, and she didn't want to take a chance on insulting her.

"Grandma's house," Gracie called out just as they rounded the corner. "Can we stop?"

"Easter Bunny," Sonia said. "He go sleep."

"Another time," Alex said, and wondered why it was so important to be on time. Maybe Sonia was like that all the time, and Alex hadn't noticed.

Again, Alex looked in the rearview mirror and saw Sonia texting.

When they got to the mall, Sonia got Gracie out of her car seat and took her hand. "We go," she said, and rushed toward the mall.

They all followed to the carousel. There were several huge costumed bunnies taking children by the hand and parading around the path in a circle. They were giving all the children little baskets. In the center, next to the carousel, there was a small farmhouse and there were several real goats and ducks near the farmhouse.

"Wash your hands right after you touch the animals," Alex said. "And do not feed them." There, Alex had taken care of every possible danger—or had she?

CHAPTER 19

Alex and Eric walked through the mall and went directly to Foot Locker. They looked at a few sneakers and found the ones Eric had shown her online. He grabbed the floor sample, and they sat down to wait for a salesperson.

Unlike the rest of the mall, Foot Locker wasn't very busy, which was unusual for the Saturday before Easter, especially when the mall was crowded. It only took five minutes for a salesperson to come over and measure Eric's feet. Then the salesperson went to the back to retrieve the sneakers in Eric's size.

"See, Mom?" Eric pointed to the Brannock foot-measuring device.

She looked over and saw he had grown an entire size. "It was a good idea to have come to the store."

They talked about his team and how happy he was in Laguna Beach—the perfect environment for him, especially since he was looking forward to surfing this summer. Alex was enjoying the time alone with him. Interesting how when the children were little, they yearned to be with their parents, savoring every minute. But when they get older, it becomes difficult for parents to steal even a few moments with them; they're so busy with school, friends, and sports.

He decided on the yellow, bright yellow, sneakers. "The same color as Gracie's little chicken stuffed animal," he joked.

"She loves that chicken," Alex agreed. Then she looked at Eric. "Should we buy the sneakers now?"

"Really?" he asked, obviously surprised since they'd agreed it would be just as easy and probably cheaper online.

"Let's get them," she said. Usually frugal, rarely impulsive, and definitely not one to spoil the children, she decided to make this a real treat for him; especially since, being Jewish, her boys wouldn't be getting Easter presents. And she was certain Cecile and Warren would be showering Gracie with gifts tomorrow, Easter Sunday. Cecile and Warren would probably bring some little things for her boys also, ignoring the fact that they didn't celebrate Easter. The main thing was David had agreed to have everyone over for Easter dinner; it was important for Gracie to have her family around, especially at holiday times. Maybe, just maybe, it could make the loss of her mother a little less painful.

"Wow." Eric took the sneakers off and placed them in the box.

She paid at the counter, delighted to see him pleased beyond his expectations. Then, they made their way back to the carousel at the center of the mall where they'd left Gracie and Jon with Sonia.

The goats were roaming around, as were the ducks. The little bunnies were scampering all over. The costumed bunnies were walking the children along the path and giving out baskets.

Jon was standing alone, crying.

Alex picked him up and held him. "Cookie Face, what happened? Why are you crying?"

"They didn't pick me."

"What are you talking about?"

"The parade," Jon said. "They picked kids to walk around with the stuffed people, and they got baskets."

Alex looked for Gracie and Sonia. When she couldn't find them, she thought they had to be in the ladies' room. "Wait here with Eric," she told Jon, and ran to the ladies' room.

"Gracie," Alex yelled as she banged on each stall door in the ladies' room. No answer. Frantic, panic gripping her, she ran back to the carousel.

"Did you lose your child?" a woman asked and offered to help.

"No. Yes. I don't know." Alex turned to Jon. "Where did Gracie and Sonia go?"

The woman who'd offered to help clutched her own child's hand and said, "We didn't see anyone take a child."

"Yes," Jon said. "A big chicken took Gracie away."

Eric shook his head. "Doofus, are you crazy?"

Panicked, Alex dialed Sonia. It went to voice mail. "Where are you?" she yelled. She started to sweat. Her heart was beating so fast she thought she'd faint. "Jon, you have to tell me what happened."

"The big bunnies were getting kids, but they didn't pick me, so—"

"Where's Gracie? Sonia?" Alex was looking feverishly at all the entryways surrounding the carousel. Then she thought of the only possibility: "Jon, did Sonia tell you she was taking Gracie to a store?"

"I told you, the big chicken took Gracie," he said between tears.

"There he goes again." Eric rolled his eyes.

Unable to fathom anything other than Gracie leaving with Sonia, Alex looked at Jon sternly. "Jon, this isn't funny. You have to think. Where did Gracie and Sonia go?"

"Mommy, I keep telling you. Gracie got picked by the big chicken, but . . ."

The woman who was with her child moved close to Alex and said, "I'm going to find mall security."

Nodding appreciatively but unable to even think of the next step, Alex whispered, "Yes." She was frantic and decided to try asking Jon in another way: "Did that big chicken say anything to Sonia or Gracie?"

"No, but Sonia said, 'Oh, my God.' Just like you always tell me I shouldn't say."

She was starting to believe him, which was making it even more terrifying. "Jon, did Sonia and Gracie go with the chicken?" she asked, piecing together a possibility even more horrific than she dared imagine.

"And Mommy, after the chicken left with Gracie, Sonia yelled at me. She said *Esperate* to me, and I didn't know if it was a bad word."

"It's not," Alex said. "Sonia was worried, so she didn't know she was speaking Spanish, and she just said a word that means *you wait.*"

Terrified, in need of answers, Alex ran up to one of the costumed bunnies.

"Where did the costumed chicken go?"

"Lady, we don't have chickens."

"There was a chicken. My son told me—"

"Lady, do you see a chicken?" he asked sarcastically. When she didn't answer, he said, "Maybe one of the bunnies ate the chicken."

"Eric," she yelled. "Go get the mall police."

Paralyzed with fear, Eric didn't move. "The woman said she was going to get the mall security."

The costumed bunny stared at her and laughed. "You're calling security 'cause we have no chickens?"

"David," she screamed.

"There's no David here either," the bunny said. "I think mall security needs to check you out."

"This isn't funny," Alex yelled. "Where's the mall security office?"

The costumed bunny pointed.

Alex grabbed Jon by the hand, told Eric to follow, and ran in the direction of the security office. Terrified, she cried out, "Where the hell is a security guard?"

"Mommy, you're not supposed to say *hell*," Jon said.

She saw the woman walking toward her with a security guard beside her. Alex ran to him. "They took my child," she screamed, and as soon as she said the word *child*, she thought of David. Fear, guilt, panic short-circuited her. It was happening too fast. She had to call David. Fingers trembling, she punched in his number.

"What's up?" David asked.

"Gracie," she screamed and started to cry. "Sonia's gone."

"Don't cry, Mommy. The big chicken will bring Gracie back." Jon looked up at her, his big brown eyes still tearful.

"Alex, talk to me. Where are you?" David asked.

The security guard folded his arms across his chest and waited.

She had to tell David what had happened, but she needed to explain everything to the security guard and make them search the mall.

"Speak," David yelled, fear resonating in his voice.

"There was a parade and Jon and Gracie were there with Sonia, and . . ."

"Alex," he said, exasperated, fearful. "You said Sonia was gone, but . . ."

She rubbed her wrist. "We . . . I—"

"Ma'am," the security guard interrupted her.

"I asked where's Gracie?" David yelled.

"Gracie's gone."

CHAPTER 20

While walking to the security office, Alex described the incident to the security guard as best she could. Eric and Jon followed silently, their fear palpable. Then the guard asked Alex to tell him what Gracie looked like.

"Beautiful," Alex said. "Gracie has long brown hair, and she was wearing a white dress, her garden dress." Every detail made the terror more real. "You've got to shut the mall exits," she screamed.

"Sorry, ma'am, we can't just close the mall until we meet certain criteria."

Panic overtaking her, she asked, "What criteria? My child is gone. What more do you need?"

"We have to be sure this is a missing child, not just a lost—"

"What the hell difference does it make?" she asked, certain she had to convince the guard this was serious, dangerous. "Please," she begged.

Her phone rang.

"David, they're searching the mall right now. They'll find her," she said, but feared it was futile. She was crazed and knew he was as well. Her mind filled with horrific thoughts, then suddenly, she remembered Daniel was home alone. She hadn't thought about asking David to bring him; her only thought was of Gracie. Now she realized someone could take Daniel too.

She called Daniel's cell and instructed him to get out of the house. She told him to go next door and wait. In answer to his questions, she barked, "Gracie's gone."

She hung up just as they got to the security office, where two Costa Mesa police officers had already been summoned.

A handsome black-haired police officer introduced himself. "I'm Sergeant Turcio, and I want to assure you our main goal is to reunite you with your child. We are asking for your cooperation, and while some of the questions are sensitive, they might help us return your child to you as swiftly as possible. Be assured we will be here twenty-four seven until we find your child."

Alex looked around the mall security office. "You're going to stay here twenty-four hours a day?" she asked, her terror becoming tangible, real. They were planning for twenty-four hours, twenty-four hours without knowing where Gracie . . . No, she couldn't even think about that, and she couldn't even imagine what David was going through as he drove to the mall. Each second had to be even more painful than the one before.

Sergeant Turcio nodded. "Be assured we'll have patrol cars out looking for your little girl once we get your preliminary description disseminated, and officers will start pulling over any suspicious cars that exit the mall. Now, we need a more detailed description. Tell us exactly what Gracie was wearing, height, weight, everything."

"Can't you shut the mall?" she begged.

"No," the sergeant said. "We're searching all the stores, the entire mall. And we announced a lost child and requested everyone stay in the mall, but we can't make them."

"Why?" she asked.

"We've already sent guards to each exit, and they'll get the phone numbers and identification from anyone who wants to leave the mall. We're in the process of setting up an Incident Command Center right here in the mall. We feel it's best here because people who come forward will know where to go. First thing is to get out a full description."

"Gracie's beautiful," Alex repeated and started to cry.

"Mommy, Gracie's going to come back to us. Don't cry." Jon took her hand.

"We need it to be as specific as possible," Sergeant Turcio said. "I know this is difficult, but we've managed many of these cases."

Alex rubbed her wrist. Yes, to him it was one of "these cases," not Gracie. She also knew no one could really know how painful it was—unless they were going through it. Even though she'd lost custody of her children and had been devastated, this was different. This loss was fraught with horrific possibilities, possibilities of harm to Gracie.

"The description, please," the sergeant said, calling her back to reality, this ghastly reality.

"I'm sorry," she said, knowing every second was critical, and she had to provide him with a detailed description. "Like I told the guard, Gracie has long brown hair, blue eyes. She was wearing a white dress with tiny pink flowers." Alex tried to stay composed. "She had white leggings. And she had a pink bow in her hair."

"Anything else?"

Alex tried to think, but the voice in her head was screaming: *Why did you leave her?* Her guilt was warring with her fear, and she fought to stay composed. "She had a pink sweater."

"Mommy, she was wearing the black shoes that you bought her," Jon said.

133

Alex pulled Jon to her. "Yes, she had black patent leather shoes."

"Any jewelry?" the sergeant asked. Then he said softly, "In case we find it on the ground, or . . ."

"She had little earrings." Alex was embarrassed to say they were diamonds. She thought it was inappropriate for a four-year-old—yes, she was four when her mother had given them to her—to have diamond earrings. It didn't matter now. Nothing mattered except getting Gracie back. She wanted her with all her heart, and wiped a tear from her cheek.

Eric went over to the desk and got her a tissue.

Jon hugged her, his lower lip starting to quiver.

"You were saying . . ." the sergeant prompted.

Alex looked at him and said, "Oh, little diamonds, very tiny."

"Before I take you each to a different room to be interviewed—"

"You're going to interview Jon without me?" She felt guilty wanting to hold on to her child when David couldn't and might never— No, she couldn't even think that. The thought of her seven-year-old boy being interviewed alone in a room with a police officer was scary for her, but anything that was needed to bring Gracie back had to be done. And she couldn't think about her child's well-being when Gracie's very life might be at stake.

"It's protocol," Sergeant Turcio said. "You'll be close and can come into the room at any time. We need to talk to him to see what he remembers and then correlate it to your account."

"Are you thinking I—"

"Definitely not. We're not thinking you're the perpetrator, but we have to get as much information as possible. It's standard."

"Standard?" Alex repeated. "Nothing about this is standard." But in a way, there really was a modicum of comfort in the protocol. There was hope, hope in their competency, hope they could really get Gracie back.

"Before we start the interviews, let me assure you there'll be at least a hundred people on this case until we find her, because—"

Eric looked at the officer. "You're getting a hundred people to—"

Sergeant Turcio nodded. "Every second counts. We've already got everything in motion. We need a picture for the Amber Alert and the press conference, and—"

"A press conference?" Eric repeated. "People will be in front of the house like—"

Alex looked at Eric sternly. "We don't care about anything except Gracie."

"The officer in charge will be holding the press conference in the station and giving out all the details: place she was last seen, hair color, eye color, ethnicity, clothing, etcetera, but we withhold the name. We have to do it quickly and ask for the public's help. And as soon as I talk to your son, I'll be sending the description of the suspected abductor to the press for dissemination."

Jon reached out to Alex. "Mommy, we have to go back to the carousel. Gracie will be there."

"Son, we can't," Sergeant Turcio said. "We have it closed off, and bloodhounds are on the way."

"You're going to have dogs there?" Eric asked.

"Yes, they're trained to track human scent."

Heart pounding and panicked, she asked in an uncharacteristically caustic tone, "Why are we talking? You need to look for Gracie."

The sergeant nodded. "My job is first and foremost to make you and your children comfortable."

"Finding Gracie would make me comfortable," Alex snapped, and then was sorry she'd used that tone, but her guard was down. She was raw, vulnerable, and scared.

"We've already called in the FBI, the fire department, surrounding police precincts, volunteers, the Red Cross, and—"

Jon shook his head. "There was no fire. I saw the big yellow chicken take Gracie, but there was no . . . We need our Gracie back."

Alex put her arm around him. "They know there's no fire."

Sergeant Turcio explained, "The fire department is in charge of supplies."

"Don't you have all the equipment?" Alex started to cry. All the details were making her head spin. This was a nightmare, and she hoped none of her thoughts were coming to fruition now, right now.

"The fire department is in charge of blankets, food, and—"

"Blankets? They're going to sleep here?" Eric asked.

The sergeant nodded. "We'll do whatever it takes to find Gracie."

CHAPTER 21

The mall security office was crowded with recent arrivals: two bloodhounds, five more police officers, and two firefighters. Jon and Eric looked terrified.

David ran into the office. He started to hug Alex, but stopped. "What happened?" he asked, just like he'd kept asking her on the phone, but she didn't have an answer. She had nothing to tell him except to repeat exactly what Jon had told her.

Then David turned to Jon. He bent down, took him by the shoulders, and looked into his eyes. "Jon, do you remember if Sonia was with anyone? Anyone," he pleaded.

"The lady from the park was there," Jon said.

"What woman?" David appeared as though he wanted to shake the information from Jon.

Alex signaled to David, beseeching him to try to be as calm as possible. She knew if Jon became frightened, he would start crying, and then he wouldn't be helpful.

"Sonia never told me her name." Jon's lower lip started to quiver.

"Think," David screamed at Jon, who started to cry.

Alex looked at her little boy, seated there being questioned, the only witness to this horrific event. She knew every minute counted, but she couldn't let David interrogate Jon like this,

137

make him feel responsible, and then if . . . No, she couldn't think of that, not now, not yet.

She went over, picked Jon up, and sat down. As she pulled him to her lap, she caught a look of disapproval from David. She wasn't trying to undermine him, but she knew keeping Jon calm was the only way they would get any information.

Usually annoyed by Jon's very presence, Eric leaned over and put his arm around his little brother. "You're the only eyewitness. You—"

"What's an eyewitness?" Jon asked.

"It means you're the only one who saw that big chicken take Gracie," Alex said. "So, they need you to tell them everything about what happened."

"What if I can't remember?"

"Jon," she whispered. "This is important."

"Mommy, you always tell me I have to pay attention when it's important, but I didn't know the parade was important." Jon teared up, ready to have a full-on meltdown.

David looked at Jon sternly, clearly not interested in any seven-year-old's reason for doing what any normal seven-year-old would do. "Please try to remember."

Jon looked at him with terror in his eyes. "It was the big chicken, like I keep telling everybody. There were a whole bunch of big bunnies. But there was only one big chicken, and the big chicken took Gracie."

David exploded. "I can't sit here and talk about a chicken." He looked at the police officer who was standing there, waiting to take Jon back to question him. "Are you doing anything?" he demanded.

"Sir, we're searching every store and restroom, all the restaurants and common areas. As I told your wife, we've placed security staff at each exit and we've already dispersed several squad cars in the area, and they're circling the mall and surrounding streets, especially the freeways."

"What, you're looking for a chicken driving a car?" David yelled.

Jon started to laugh, but Alex cautioned him. "This is serious. Gracie could . . ." She couldn't even articulate her fears. She thought of Gracie. They'd all been so busy with the details of how it happened, how they were going to find her, that they hadn't even allowed themselves to really think about Gracie. How frightened she must be. What must be going on in her mind? And of course, the dreaded question: What were they doing to her? What would happen to her if they didn't find her quickly?

"Jon, you know how much we all love Gracie, and the answers you give could help us find her," David said. "You're the most important person in the whole world for Gracie right now."

Jon shook his head. "She loves you the best. She told me."

Alex got up and stood near David, ready to reach out to him, to comfort him, but she knew nothing short of Gracie's return would placate him.

Sergeant Turcio turned to David. "We need some information before we put out an Amber Alert."

"What's that?" David wiped a tear from his eye.

"Amber stands for America's Missing: Broadcast Emergency Response," the security guard said.

"I don't give a shit what Amber Alert stands for. I meant what information do you need from me?"

Sergeant Turcio said, "We're going to alert the Department of Transportation and interrupt regular radio and TV programming. We need a picture to verify all the particulars your wife gave us such as age, height, weight, hair color, eye—"

"Long brown hair, blue eyes, four feet, fifty pounds. Here's a picture." David held out his cell phone. "Now find her."

Eric and Jon sat in the corner, wide-eyed.

Sergeant Turcio looked at the picture. "We have to meet certain criteria first, and—"

"What fucking criteria? My daughter is missing. What more do you need?"

"We need to be sure this isn't just a lost child. We need proof that the child is in danger, and . . ."

"Are you fucking kidding me? The child's in danger." David almost reached out and grabbed the sergeant by the shoulders. "Jon told you, she didn't wander away. Someone took her."

Sergeant Turcio moved back and said, "We're going to call in the Child Abduction Response Team to help you."

"I need you to help me now, not some team."

"David," Alex whispered, trying to comfort him but knowing it was impossible. Like a caged animal, he was ready to pounce. She'd never seen him like that, but then again, his child had never been in danger. To David, Gracie was everything.

Eric leaned over and put his arm around Jon, an unusual gesture that Alex knew was partially out of empathy but also out of fear, fear that something terrible was happening to his family.

"Okay," David said, trying to calm down but failing. "What's your 'team' going to do?"

The sergeant touched David's sleeve. It was an innocent gesture, but David winced and pulled back.

Sergeant Turcio put his hand in his pocket. "CART, Child Abduction Response Team, calls in—"

"Is every fucking thing an acronym?"

As though he didn't hear him, the sergeant continued. "We have investigators and forensic experts, crime intelligence analysts, as well as trained volunteers who've had a child in a similar situation, and—"

"I don't want to talk to a volunteer who has gone through this. I don't want to go through this. I—"

Sergeant Turcio nodded. "Before the officer starts to question you, we should report this to the NCMEC, and—"

"Another fucking acronym. What is that supposed to mean?" David screamed.

"NCMEC is the National Center for Missing and Exploited Children, 1-800-THE-LOST."

"That's encouraging," David said sarcastically.

"They've blocked off the crime scene, and we have officers who are interviewing people at the scene right now."

CHAPTER 22

David started to leave the mall security office.

A police officer rushed over to him and asked, "Where are you going?"

"I'm going to rip the bunnies' costumes off and ask them what happened."

Sergeant Turcio stopped him. "I told you, we have the entire area by the carousel cordoned off, and we're interrogating people at the scene right now."

"I need to find her," David said. "Gracie," he screamed—a sound too loud for the little office, a sound that was terrifying, a sound that was so urgent it was visceral.

"Sir, we have officers all over the mall," Sergeant Turcio assured him.

The other police officer signaled to Alex. "Please follow me."

She looked at Eric and Jon. "I can't just leave them here."

David's head almost snapped back, he turned so quickly. "You can't leave them, but you left Gracie?"

"I left her with Sonia," Alex said, but she knew nothing would ever make that okay—except Gracie. She bent down and instructed Eric, "Stay here with Jon and don't go anywhere."

"We're going to interrogate the parents first and then the children," Turcio said to the other officer.

"I don't want to be the interrogation." Jon started to cry.

"I'll be back in a few minutes," Alex promised, remembering an hour ago when she said that to him. That time she thought he and Gracie would be fine with Sonia.

The police officers took David to one room and Alex to another while the boys waited outside.

Alex went into the back office, sat down across from the police officer, and answered every question, heart pounding, fearing for Gracie. In minute detail, she described their trip to the mall.

When the officer asked whether there was anything out of the ordinary, she insisted life had been calm, perfect. And when he asked whether Gracie had been on the internet recently, Alex reminded him she was six. He'd explained age was irrelevant.

Then he asked, "Was the child's behavior normal?" She assured him she and David were attentive, loving parents. They weren't irresponsible, but here they were.

"Are there custody issues?" he asked, and then explained, "Over fifty percent of these abductions are family members who want their children back."

"Mother died," she said, sure that would explain it had to be a stranger, someone who could be doing terrible things to Gracie right now. Alex's mind flashed to *Room,* a movie they'd just seen about a girl who was abducted and made a sex slave for seven years before she escaped. She started to sweat.

The officer nodded. "So, you're not the mother?"

"I'm her stepmother," Alex said. True, it was different, but she loved Gracie. Recently, when David was at the hospital late at night and couldn't put Gracie to bed, Alex would go to Gracie's room and read her a story. Then they'd cuddle in bed, whispering about girl things. Alex even told her silly stories about when she was a little girl, and they'd laugh together.

Alex and Gracie were referred to as the girls in the family. They'd share knowing smiles when the boys in the family did bad things like run upstairs with dirty sneakers or shoes with cleats. Yes, those were the bad things; that was, up until now.

"Do you, or did you have custody issues?"

Alex panicked, wondering how she was going to explain her former husband and she had a custody battle so poisonous it threatened to become murderous. Yes, her former husband had tried to have her killed, but how could that have anything to do with Gracie?

"Custody issues?" the officer repeated.

She told him there was a custody issue, but she left out the part about him hiring a man to divert and then eventually destroy her. She also left out the part about him twisting the truth and accusing her of purposefully burning Jon. There was no reason to reveal that; it would just make the officer suspicious of her, convince him she'd been irresponsible in the past and might have also been today.

Gabe needed money now for his trials but would he ever... well, could she really say what he was capable of? True, he'd done one horrendous thing after another. Would he ever stoop to something as evil as taking Gracie? Her mind was going to horrific dark places. She even thought maybe, just maybe, he could have kidnapped Gracie and was going to demand ransom. No, she decided that was crazy.

The officer then asked, "Was there someone who paid her lots of attention recently?"

"No," she whispered, but she knew Cecile and Warren always showered Gracie with gifts and treated her special. There didn't seem any reason to mention that even though the officer had alluded to relatives abducting . . . No, there was no reason to say anything about Cecile or Warren.

Then he asked about timing. He explained they had surveillance cameras throughout the mall and had to know the exact time, so they could check the videos.

But Alex also knew the more time that passed, the worse it was for finding Gracie. She recalled they'd arrived at the mall at 3:10. That was because Sonia seemed worried she was late, and her new friend wouldn't be there. Alex had been so pleased Sonia had made a friend so quickly, and it seemed Sonia was worried about annoying her friend.

The officer asked Alex what time the girl disappeared.

Alex looked down at her lap, guilty, nervous that he'd judge her as an irresponsible parent. She really had no idea what time Gracie had left Sonia's care. "I don't know," she answered.

"What do you mean? Weren't you there?"

Alex shook her head. It took every ounce of restraint for her to sit there instead of running into the mall and calling for Gracie. Instead, she answered, "Like I told the security guard, I left Gracie and Jon, my son, with Sonia, the nanny, while I went shopping with—"

"Where did you go shopping?" the officer asked.

She could hear David in the other room, yelling, begging the officer to find his daughter. She wanted to go to him, comfort him, but in truth, she had no idea what to say to make the pain lessen.

"Where did you go?" the officer repeated.

"I took the oldest, Eric, to Foot Locker to buy sneakers." There, she said it. It seemed so trite, so irresponsible now.

"So, you left the two little children with the nanny and took the oldest to shop?"

"Yes," she whispered. It wasn't like that, it really wasn't. Sonia was hired to watch the children. Sonia was even going to take Gracie to the mall herself before Alex had offered to join them. Alex wondered what would have happened if she'd stayed home. No, Gracie was gone. It didn't matter whether she was there or not. Nothing mattered except finding Gracie.

"How long did you leave the children?" he asked.

"I left for . . ." She couldn't really remember. She had to think backwards. "It was 3:10 when we got to the mall. Then, Eric and I went for the sneakers. We probably left Gracie and Jon with Sonia at 3:15." She took a breath, "We . . . The shoes . . . It was only forty-five minutes, but . . ."

"Yes?"

She started to cry. "I think we waited too long. We didn't believe Jon, so I thought, I mean, I thought Sonia took Gracie to the bathroom. I didn't—"

"We need to show something to your son, the one who was there." The officer got up and went to the front. "Get the grid up," he instructed the security guard.

As David came back to the front room, she heard him implore the officer, "Please, we can't sit here, and—"

The security guard who was seated at the front desk looked up from the screen and said, "We're trying to get the grid up and see if we can find her and . . ."

David rushed over to look at the computer screen. As though willing the frame to freeze, go back to a time when Gracie was just a little girl who was excited to see the Easter Bunny, he stared at the screen.

"There she is," David said and watched Gracie leave the carousel area with someone in a yellow chicken costume.

"We have well-placed cameras, but now they're off the grid," the security guard said.

"Wait, look at that frame," David pointed to the bathroom entrance. A man in a chicken costume was entering the bathroom. "What happened?"

"We don't have cameras in the bathroom."

Sergeant Turcio called Jon to come and look at the screen. He had Jon sit in the security officer's chair and asked, "See the big chicken? Is that the one you saw?"

Then Jon started to cry. He looked up at the sergeant and begged, "You need to find our Gracie now."

"We're trying," the sergeant said.

David looked at the screen again, turned to Jon, and yelled, "Was that the chicken?"

"That's Gracie's chicken," Jon said.

"Gracie's not with the chicken when he enters the men's room," Alex said. She didn't know whether that was a good thing or a horrific, unimaginable thing. "Where could Gracie have gone?"

David looked at the screen. "Maybe this whole chicken thing is . . . Wait, there's a person in a bunny costume coming out of the bathroom."

"That's the bunny who didn't pick me," Jon said.

"Now we've got a whole fucking menagerie to find." David put his head in his hands. "This is too much." He looked at Alex.

One officer said, "That's why we have to make sure the child was abducted and not just lost."

"I'm telling you the child was abducted. You think a chicken or bunny or whatever the fuck taking a child is normal?"

CHAPTER 23

While Jon and Eric were taken to the back offices for questioning, the sergeant went up to Alex and David and told them he had to ask one more thing. Alex looked at David, certain he was going to lose the already tenuous hold on his temper. He wasn't a volatile man, but then again, his entire world hadn't been shaken—until now.

"We need your permission to search the house," Sergeant Turcio said.

"Our house?" David yelled. "Why the hell would you be concerned with the house? I just left home, and—"

"We actually suggest you take the family to a hotel . . ."

A tear fell onto David's cheek. "What family? Gracie's my family."

"A hotel?" Alex repeated. "Why?"

Sergeant Turcio looked at Alex first, then David. "For the safety of the family, and—"

"Safety?" David yelled. "What safety?"

The sergeant nodded, as though he understood David's pain, but he didn't; no one could. "We don't know what this person wants, and—"

"He wants my Gracie." There was rage, raw anger, terror in David's words.

"Do we have your permission to search your home?" Sergeant Turcio repeated. "There's a chance, even though the nanny's not answering her cell phone, she might have taken the child home."

Now Gracie was referred to as *the child*. Alex was sure, for them, making it as impersonal as possible was the only way to handle it, but for her and David it was personal, too personal.

"Search the fucking mall," David said. "That's what you should do."

"That's what we're doing," the sergeant said as David signed the release giving the police permission to search their house. He would have signed anything, allowed the police to go through everything and anything.

As soon as Eric and Jon came back to the waiting area, Alex told them they were going home.

"What about Gracie?" Jon asked—the question they'd been asking over and over without any answers.

"They're going to find her," Alex said, praying that was true.

She turned to David. "Can you drive, or should I ask Liz to have her husband drive her to the mall and pick up my car?" she asked, worried about him, fearful he was too distraught to focus.

He shook his head. "You drive. I need to call Child Rescue to get everyone in the organization to help. They'll do something, not this chickenshit . . ." He stopped. The very word *chicken* probably reminded him of Chicken Love, Gracie's favorite. He wiped a tear from his eye.

Alex gave her car keys to the security guard at the desk, and they were escorted out of the mall.

They all piled into David's car, the empty car seat now a horrific reminder that Gracie was gone. As Alex drove, David called one of the board members of Child Rescue. He was trying to be coherent, but emotion was overtaking him. Exasperated, he screamed, "I need everyone, even the SEALs."

Jon scrunched up his nose. "Are the seals going to bring Gracie back?"

"No," Alex said. "David means the people who work with his organization, the people who do rescues."

"Sea, air, and land is what it stands for," Eric said.

"Good." Jon nodded. "Because Gracie's not a good swimmer."

Eric whispered something to Jon, probably trying to explain a little about SEALs, do something to take Jon's mind off of Gracie. Eric's newfound kindness toward his brother had to have emanated from knowing Jon had witnessed the loss of Gracie. A wonderful by-product, but definitely not worth their pain and terror.

As David spoke on the phone, he stared out the window, trying to peer into passing cars as though searching, checking, hoping, but knowing it was futile.

When they pulled up to their driveway, they saw the Laguna Beach police had been called in as well. There were four police cars lined up in the semicircular driveway and two officers were standing by the front door. David bolted out of the car and rushed to the door.

They heard Lucky barking from within the house.

"Lucky's scared too," Jon said.

Alex knew he'd seen and heard too much today, but she was certain his fear was infinitesimal compared to Gracie's at this moment. Her heart ached for Gracie.

One officer approached Alex's car and signaled for her to open her window. "You can't go in there until we've done a preliminary search of the premises," he said.

"Are they going to make us sleep out here all night?" Jon asked.

She almost smiled, but her sadness was too great to take any pleasure in anything, even Jon's naivety. "No," she said. "They'll just be a few minutes, then we can go in."

Eric offered Jon a stick of gum. "Calms my nerves when I play ball."

"Thanks," she said to Eric, appreciating him for his little gesture, knowing he, too, feared for Gracie.

"Should I call Daniel and tell him to come home?" Eric asked as he took out his cell phone.

"Please," she said, almost guiltily—she who had all her children safe.

She looked over and saw an officer holding David back, refusing to let him enter the house until they cleared it. And since David had given the officers permission to enter the premises, several were already inside.

Alex knew David wanted to, needed to, run to Gracie's room, but an officer blocked his entry. Then he finally opened the door for David and signaled to Alex.

As she walked toward the house, she heard David yell, "Gracie." Then his scream grew louder and louder until it was a wail. But the only other sound was his echo, his hollow echo without response.

One police officer was searching the kitchen, going through the drawers, and another one was in the family room. She knew David was upstairs and rushed to him.

He was sitting in a chair in Gracie's room, watching as two other police officers were checking the room. They searched each and every drawer and went through her closet—all her lovely dresses thrown into the bag. They inspected every doll and stuffed animal.

Hanging on the armoire, waiting for Easter, was Gracie's new pink ruffled dress, the one she and Alex had picked out together when they went to the mall, when the mall wasn't a dangerous place, a place where children weren't safe. Alex's chest tightened, recalling how excited Gracie had been about the dress, how she'd told her grandma Cecile she was going to wear her beautiful ballerina dress to church when they went to the Easter service.

"Look at this." One officer held up his gloved hand with Gracie's beloved mama chicken with the baby chick attached.

David reached out to take the stuffed chicken. "Chicken Love is her favorite . . ."

The officer held on to the stuffed animal and then dropped it into the big plastic bag. "Who else knew she had this?"

"She wanted to take it to the mall, but we're trying to wean her off taking it everywhere." David fought back tears. "I told her I needed Chicken Love to keep me company while she went to the mall."

"That's why the stuffing is coming out," Alex said. It didn't really matter. Frightened, standing there in Gracie's room, she thought about how much Gracie needed her Chicken Love now, right now. The reality was staring her in the face, and she couldn't turn away. Gracie wasn't coming home tonight or . . .

"Wanna see my room?" Jon asked from the doorway.

She knew he was trying to help, but even the sound of her child, safe, was unnerving. Silence was the only respectful noise here in Gracie's room.

The officer patted Jon's head. "In a while."

"Why are you taking her stuff?" Jon asked. "Are you going to bring it to her?"

The officer put Chicken Love in the bag. "We have to take it for her scent."

"Mom," Daniel called from downstairs.

She ran downstairs to him. "It's bad," she said, and could see he'd been crying. She hugged him, relieved he was okay.

"Most abductions occur within a quarter mile of the child's home," Daniel said.

She knew from the moment she called him, he'd read everything about child abduction. His way of coping was to find out everything about the situation. Yes, it was now a "situation."

"Actually," Daniel continued. "Fifty percent of kidnappings are family members, twenty-seven percent are acquaintances, and only twenty-three percent are strangers."

"You're telling me it could be someone who knows Gracie? No, it's not possible." Alex couldn't fathom the possibility someone she knew, someone they knew would do such a cruel thing. *Gabe*, she thought, and then dismissed it as ridiculous.

"Mom." Daniel looked at her. "Mall kidnappings are . . ."

"Tell me," she demanded. She knew he'd already researched everything about abductions, kidnappings, whatever. That was how he dealt with life—facts helped him cope.

"The 1975 case of Katherine and Sheila Lyon, the sisters who were abducted from a mall in Maryland by a man who'd served a prison sentence for sexual abuse of children . . ."

"What?" she begged, fearing the answer, but needing to know.

He shook his head, and she knew what that meant. Then he told her about the 1981 mall kidnapping of Adam Walsh, abducted from a mall in Hollywood, Florida, while waiting to play the Atari 2600 game at Sears.

Then obviously trying to change the subject, he said, "South Coast Plaza mall is the largest mall on the West Coast and has twenty-four million visitors a year, so . . ."

As though willing the nightmare to end, she closed her eyes and shook her head. "So, one of twenty-four million people could have taken Gracie."

Jon came downstairs to the vestibule and hugged his brother. "Glad they didn't take you too."

"Do they think it was Sonia?" Daniel asked his mother.

"We have no idea. She's gone too. They're looking for her."

Jon tugged on his brother's sleeve. "I think Sonia didn't watch us like she was supposed to."

Alex nodded sadly. "But there are sometimes bad people out there, people we don't know and—"

David's cell phone started to ring. She reached for it on the kitchen table. The caller ID showed it was Cecile. She answered. "I'll get David for you."

Jon followed as she went upstairs and handed the phone to David.

"Cecile, I know. We will . . ." He broke down.

Alex took the phone. "They're looking right now. Yes, I know the Amber Alert went out." She listened to Cecile, her pain palpable. "I don't know." She handed the phone back to David.

He grabbed the phone and listened. "No. You don't have to have Warren drive you here tonight. It's too late. Come over tomorrow." He handed it back to Alex and shook his head.

She covered the phone. "Cecile needs you too."

"I can't help her. Gracie's gone." He fell to the floor. Then he reached into the plastic bag and grabbed the bright yellow stuffed animal. "Chicken Little, the sky is really falling."

The police officer took the stuffed animal from David and returned it to the bag.

Jon shook his head. "Gracie calls her Chicken Love, not Chicken Little."

David scowled. "Who gives a shit what the chicken's . . ."

Jon's lips quivered, and he scampered out of the room.

"Gracie's not dead. I'm sure of that," Alex said.

"How can you know?" He wiped a tear from his eye. "The longer she's gone, the—"

"I'm so sorry I trusted Sonia," she said, and then realized her feelings didn't matter. She had her children and could only imagine how horrific it was for David. She went to hug him. There were no words that would make his pain any less intense. She had loss and guilt, but he had a part of himself ripped away and nothing could fill the hole in his heart.

"Parents' room next," the other officer said.

"Are we suspects?" David asked caustically. She knew he was angry they were wasting time looking here when his little girl was out there, out in the world, alone.

CHAPTER 24

While the police were busy wiretapping the phone, putting up surveillance cameras, and searching the upstairs bedrooms, David went downstairs, walked to the family room, and took out an album.

Alex followed him. "They're going to find Gracie," she repeated.

"Alex, you can do better than that."

Jon came running into the family room. "There's a helicopter outside."

"This is only the beginning." David started looking at pictures.

Daniel opened the front door. "The police are all over the neighborhood."

Just as Jon was going toward the door, Alex pulled him close to her. "Stay in the house."

"Mommy, what's going on?" Jon squirmed away and ran to the window. "Now are the helicopters bringing Gracie back to us and not the seals?"

"Soon, very soon, because when bad people take children, they return them." She lied, but decided there was no need to make him worry even more—that was, until . . . until Gracie was . . . No, she couldn't even think about that.

"But, Mommy, do the bad people take lots of children?"

"No, Jon, children aren't usually taken," she said. But in truth, she knew they really were; children were taken often, more often than she wanted to think about.

"Wrong," Daniel said. "Every forty seconds a child goes missing according to the National Center for Missing and Exploited Children, NCMEC, the organization founded by Adam Walsh's parents. That's the kid who was taken in a mall in Florida, and ..."

Alex didn't want to talk in front of Jon, but she had to know what he'd learned, what he knew, whether knowing would help. "How many do they find?"

Daniel shook his head. "According to ERASE Child Trafficking Organization, there are seventeen hundred children who are abducted in the United States every year. That's forty-six every school day—two full classrooms don't return home each day, and ..."

"And I want one, just one," David said, weakly, broken. Then he looked up from the album. "Do we have to listen to his statistics? Child Rescue did an operation in Peru and rescued fifty girls. And they didn't have funds to house the girls, so do you know where they put them? In a jail. A jail was the only place they could use to house the girls, and—"

"Is Gracie in jail like where my daddy's going?" Jon asked.

Alex pulled Jon to her. She whispered in his ear, imploring him to try to understand how serious this was, how Gracie was going to come back home soon, very soon.

David slammed the album shut. "And where's the FBI that they said they called in?"

"The FBI used to be called only if it was an interstate problem, but now they are involved if a minor's in danger," Daniel said, softly, obviously hoping this information would help.

The doorbell rang.

As Alex opened the door, she saw a police van parked on the curb across the street.

"We're here for you." Liz held Alex, who started to cry. With her First Friday Book Club women here, she no longer had to be strong.

Meredith and Terrie followed. Embracing Alex, they offered words of encouragement. Then Meredith went directly into the family room. "David, Warren's waiting in the car. He'd like to come in."

"Let him," David said. "I have no strength to argue. I know he's hurting too. We're all . . ." He choked up, unable to speak.

"Boys," Terrie called. "You have to eat." She started to unpack the bag of food she'd brought from Mangione's Restaurant. "Spaghetti and meatballs."

"Thanks, but I'm not hungry," Daniel said, and returned his attention to his laptop.

"You really should eat," Alex said, and called Eric down.

Warren walked in, looking like he'd been crying.

David embraced him. Maybe it was guilt, guilt for robbing him of his niece, or maybe he needed family, any family, even one he hated.

"I'm so sorry," Warren said. "What can I do?"

"Warren," Alex said. "You should be with Cecile. She's hysterical."

"I know," he said. "I've been on the phone with her ever since she heard what happened. She wanted to come over, but I told her to wait till tomorrow if . . ." He turned to Alex. "Why would anyone send a little girl to the mall with a brand-new au pair?"

Meredith looked at Warren, cautioning him, and said, "Dear, this is not the time for judgment."

Liz nodded. "We're here to give support."

"Should we make posters?" Terrie asked. "I can start."

Daniel looked up from his computer. "The NCMEC already has them in process."

"What's that?" Warren asked.

"Acronyms are my new hobby." David turned and started back toward the family room, instructing, "Daniel, tell him."

Daniel accepted a plate of food. "National Center for Missing and Exploited Children. They review and analyze all the leads and then get them to the local investigating law enforcement, and they have volunteers who've had a child in their own family in this situation."

"Right," David called from the family room. "Like I want to talk to some other freaked-out parent."

Terrie put her arms around Alex. "I'm sure talking to someone who's been through it will help and will provide great emotional support."

Eric sat down at the table and tentatively accepted a plate of spaghetti and meatballs from Terrie. Obviously emotional, he said, "That's Gracie's second-favorite dinner."

"Mac and cheese is first," Alex said. She knew now everything would be measured in before Gracie was gone and after.

Terrie offered to serve Alex, who refused. "You must eat."

She couldn't eat, not when she didn't know where Gracie was, whether she'd ever have her favorite dinner again.

"We can't just sit here," Warren said. "What're they doing?"

The two police officers who'd been searching Sonia's room downstairs walked into the kitchen. "We didn't find a phone or any other—"

"She has her cell phone with her at all times, but she's not answering it," Alex said.

"Tell us everything you know about her," the officer said. "Where would she go?"

"Sonia was so nice," Eric said. "Do you really think she'd take Gracie?"

Daniel fought back tears. "Colombia is known for trafficking, and they—"

"I know that very well," David said, and he walked back to the kitchen. "Child Rescue busted a huge trafficking ring in Colombia last year."

"No," Jon said. "Sonia told me where she lived in Colombia, there weren't lots of cars."

Alex looked at Daniel, cautioning him not to say anything about trafficking. She didn't want Jon to hear more about the horrific things people were capable of, things a child should never know.

CHAPTER 25

As Alex walked Warren and the First Friday Book Club women to the door, she saw the police were still outside. Then there was no one in the house except the family. The family . . . *Were they still a family now that one was missing?*

"Could we believe anything Sonia said?" David wondered aloud. "And we picked her."

"I'm sorry," Alex said, feeling more than just terror and fear, a feeling that was compounded by guilt and blame. It was as though hiring Sonia was her fault, her fault for having a practice, a practice that took her away from the children, made her an irresponsible mother. No, she had fought those feelings during her own custody battle. Now, she needed to face the most horrific of all possibilities a parent could imagine. Now, she needed to be strong, strong enough for both herself and David because his life, their life, Gracie's life was now tenuous.

David went back to the family room, picked up another album, and sat down.

Alex followed him into the room and stood at the entryway, watching him move his hand across the page as though he could will Gracie back by stroking her face.

161

Then he screamed, a scream that was so guttural, so horrific it had a color, a scent, a taste, even a texture. It was red, bright red, acrid, bitter, rough. She wondered whether he'd screamed like that when he'd learned Harper was dead. He slammed the album shut. "I'm going to the mall."

"David, it's closed, and they won't let you in."

"I can't sit here and wait."

"The police told us they're circling the area, and they'll call the minute they find anything."

"I'm going." He got up and started for the garage.

"I'm coming with you."

"You stay here, Alex. What if someone's watching us, waiting?"

"There are police outside, circling the area, watching."

He glared at her. "Great job they're doing scrutinizing us instead of . . . Do you know what could be happening to her?"

"David, you can't drive in this state."

She went upstairs to tell Eric they were going, instructing him to listen for Jon. Then she got the car keys and drove David to the mall, the police car that had been parked in front of their house following them all the way.

Shocked, she looked toward the shopping center across the street from the South Coast Plaza mall where the carousel was located. There were people running all around the parking lot, at least ten police cars with sirens blasting and lights beaming, and twenty or more souped-up cars were gunning their engines so loudly it was deafening.

"Oh, God," David yelled. Excitement and joy in his voice, he said, "They found Gracie. I'm going to get her. Pull over."

As soon as she stopped, he jumped out of the car and ran across the street. She watched him run through the parking lot, going from car to car. Worried he'd get hit, she drove into the lot.

A police car pulled right in front of her car, signaling her to stop. An officer got out and walked up to her. He told her to roll down the window.

She did.

"What are you doing here?" he asked.

"My child was abducted," she said. Well, she thought, Gracie was really David's child, but that didn't matter now. "Did they find Gracie?"

"We have the Amber Alert for her, but—"

"Then why are all the police cars here?" she asked.

The police officer pointed to several weird-looking cars and trucks with huge wheels. "This is just one of those burnout shows, and . . ."

Disappointment gripping her to the core, she asked, "What's a burnout show?"

"It's one of those meetings where the guys with the mod-ded-out cars post on Instagram and then assemble at a site and burn up their tires, and—"

"Why do you allow that?" she asked.

The officer shook his head. "We don't, but for now, they own the street."

"Officer," Alex said. "My husband is running around from car to car, searching for our daughter."

"He could get killed by a reckless driver," the officer said. "There are a lot of crazies out here, and that's why we have to respond."

As she spotted David running between two cars, she said, "There he is."

"Lady, he's going to get killed if he doesn't get on the sidewalk."

Alex looked at the officer. "I have to get him."

The officer tightened his lips. "I've seen distraught parents who've gone off the deep end when—"

"No," Alex whispered and started to cry.

David must have seen the officer leaning into the car because he came running back. "Did you find her?" he shouted at the officer.

"I was telling your wife this is one of those meetings where the guys with the modded-out cars post on Instagram and then assemble at a site and burn up their tires, and—"

"What the hell are you talking about?" David grabbed the officer's shoulders and glared at him. "My daughter was abducted, and you're meeting here with all the patrol cars with a group of kids who are gunning their engines?"

"We have to respond to this." The officer pushed David's hands away and reached for his baton. "We can't take a chance on hundreds of kids meeting here without dispersing them. When we get calls, we have to respond."

"I need you to find my Gracie," David screamed, a gut-wrenching plea for help.

The police officer said, "Sir, I understand your—"

"You understand nothing." David went to grab him. "Is your daughter safe at home? Huh? You don't—"

"Please," the officer said. "Go home and let us handle this."

David crumpled to the ground. "You're not—"

"We've been circling, but this call came in, and we have to monitor the crowd."

"My daughter is being raped or worse right now while you..." David yelled at the officer who was trying to help him from the ground.

CHAPTER 26

As soon as they returned home from the mall, Alex went to the kitchen to make David a cup of tea. She had to offer him something, anything that might ease some of his fear.

David refused. He just sat in his chair in the family room and stared out the glass doors at the ocean, as though willing Gracie to appear.

Alex suggested he sleep.

He refused, and she understood. No, she hadn't slept one peaceful night when her children were taken from her. Sure, they'd been safe with their father, but even now, she could feel the stab of pain, the pain she'd felt each night as she walked through the empty house. Then she'd go to Jon's room and smell his pillow, wishing for him and the older boys. Would David wander into Gracie's room tonight, she wondered. And would that give him any comfort, or would it break his heart even more?

He turned on his computer and watched video after video of Gracie. She knew he wanted to crawl into the scene and hug Gracie, make her come back.

"Can I get you anything?" she asked. She felt his fear to her core, and knew he had to be going to places so dark it would terrify any parent.

"You can get me my daughter."

"I can't," she whispered, wishing she could.

Then he laughed.

"Why are you laughing?" she asked, fearful he was cracking, that this was too much for him to bear.

He told her tonight he'd planned to take them all out for ice cream. He was going to tell them to pile into his car, then he'd start to drive. It was a simple surprise, but now, it was an impossibility, one that cut as sharp as a knife. He told her he thought about how Gracie would squeal when she guessed where they were going. It was painful, too painful.

"David, I understand—"

"How can you understand?"

"Please come upstairs." She touched his shoulder.

He pulled away. "I've got to speak to one of the SEALs from Child Rescue. He told me to call any hour, day or night." He looked at her. "All those nameless, faceless children who've been abducted and then saved by Child Rescue. Now, it's my child, and . . ." He dialed and even though it was three o'clock in the morning in New York, he knew there'd be someone to speak to and, he hoped, someone who could give him an answer.

She went upstairs, walked into Jon's room, and kissed his forehead. She sat down on his bed and pulled the cover up to his chin. "I love you," she whispered, guilty for having her baby safe.

Then she walked to Daniel's room and gingerly opened his door and listened to him sleep, grateful for every breath he took. Quietly, she peeked into Eric's room and a tear ran down her cheek. They were all safe.

As she walked past Gracie's room, her heart nearly stopped. She went into Gracie's room and sat on her bed; Gracie's beloved Chicken Love was gone, put in a plastic bag and taken to the police station for scent recognition. The quiet was unsettling. Then she looked up at the armoire. The beautiful pink Easter dress, too, was gone. Gone, and so was Gracie. The emptiness palpable, Alex started to cry.

She was uncertain of the time that had passed, and it took all her strength to pull herself away from Gracie's room. She went to her bedroom, crawled into bed, and waited for sleep to take her away from this nightmare. But neither the safety of her children nor sleep could take her away. She closed her eyes and saw beautiful Gracie, then her mind filled with thoughts of Gracie so horrific it took her breath away. She started to sweat and felt pain in the pit of her stomach and her chest tightened.

She decided to go downstairs to be with David, hold him, tell him things would be okay. But then she heard him open the door. As soon as he entered the room, she went to hug him.

He pulled away.

She understood and wondered how you could ever receive a hug when your child was in danger—needing a hug. How could you ever do anything life-affirming, pleasurable? She touched him again, this time even more gently, trying to soften his pain.

He started to cry.

"How could I have let her go to a mall?" he asked. "A mall," he yelled. "I should have gone with her."

She knew he, too, had to feel irresponsible, guilty. Guilt on top of loss—a burden too great to bear. "You can't blame your-self," she said, but she blamed herself. She'd been going over everything in minute detail, wondering whether she could have prevented it, whether there was a clue she'd missed, whether . . .

"Harper," he said. "I promised Harper. I was left with Gracie to care for, and I failed. Once Harper was diagnosed and her death was imminent, I swore Gracie would be my first, my only . . ."

"You're an amazing father . . ."

"Without my child."

She took his hand. "David, I'm letting you know I'm here, and while I love Gracie too, I can only dimly imagine your pain."

"No, Alex, you can't know my pain. You have your children."

"There was a time . . ." She stopped. She didn't need to remind him about the time she'd lost custody of her children. No, as painful as it was, she'd known they were safe. It was different.

"Something terrible is happening to Gracie," he said. "I can feel it."

"I love you," she said. There was nothing else to say, nothing that would quiet his terror. Yes, this nightmare was holding them in its arms and squeezing the life out of them, making them face a possibility too horrific to imagine.

He sat down on the bed and reached out to her.

CHAPTER 27

The next morning was Easter Sunday, but it didn't matter. Gracie's Easter dress was in a bag at the police station. Alex took the roast she'd bought out of the refrigerator and just stared at it. She started to ask David whether she should proceed with the Easter dinner for Cecile, Meredith, and Warren as planned, but she knew it was pointless to ask him what she should do. He'd just tell her to do whatever she wanted; it didn't matter. Nothing mattered now.

Daniel came downstairs and set up his computer on the kitchen table. He called to Alex, "Mom, come and listen to this."

Alex went to him and put her hand on his shoulder. Peering over at his laptop screen, she asked, "What is it?"

"Mom, it's weird. Remember I told you about the two girls in the 1975 kidnapping in that mall in Maryland who'd gone to see an Easter exhibit, and . . ."

"Easter," she repeated and rubbed her wrist. "You told me about them, but . . ."

"Their remains were never found, but the case was solved in 2013, and . . ." He looked at her. "Never mind." He shut his laptop.

Panic gripped her. The nightmare was getting more and more frightening with each passing minute. Time was moving, and

169

they weren't getting any closer to finding Gracie. That wasn't a good thing, but maybe it meant Gracie was still alive. She didn't know what to think.

She went into the dining room. No longer a place where celebratory dinners would be served, it was now the "information center." Since the neighborhood had organized people to monitor information at all times, there were four neighbors who'd come over early this morning. Four computers were open on the dining room table, and people were reviewing any and all leads.

Between the computers, a myriad of dishes filled with food donated by several restaurants in the area were carelessly strewn all over the dining room table. The expensive mahogany table, once so carefully covered with protective pads, was now cluttered with items that could scratch and mar its glistening finish. But it seemed there was no need to protect something as unimportant as a table when they'd failed to protect their child.

She went to the family room to sit near David. He'd been watching video after video of Gracie. Then without realizing it, he called out, "Gracie."

Jon ran into the room. "You said, 'Gracie.' Are we getting her back?"

Alex didn't want to fill his head with what really happened, all the evil in the world; he'd have plenty of time to learn about that.

"Cookie Face." Alex gave him a big hug. Then she looked over at David. Loving, natural gestures were now too painful for him to endure. Guiltily, she kissed his forehead. "Gracie will come back soon."

Jon shook his head. "I hope it won't be like Honey, my best dog in the whole world, 'cause Honey only comes back when I sleep."

"Jon, you know Honey's in heaven," she said.

"My Honey comes back to me in the night." Jon furrowed his brow and his lower lip started to quiver. "Is Gracie in heaven?"

"No," she said, hoping she was telling him the truth. She'd told him sometimes when people have lost the ones they've loved, they sometimes came back to visit them in their dreams, but that wasn't going to happen to Gracie. "She'll come back. I promise."

David looked up. He'd been sitting in his chair, leaning his head on his hand as though it was too heavy to hold up, the burden too great to bear.

David's phone rang.

Alex jumped up and answered his phone. She listened and whispered, "Police," to David.

"What are they saying?" David asked.

"They found Sonia," Alex said softly, trying to make it a good thing instead of the terrible reality.

"Sonia," David repeated, his tone sharp and scathing as though the name burned his throat. He bolted out of his chair and grabbed the phone out of her hand. He listened and then hung up.

When she asked him what the police had said, he threw his phone onto the chair. "Sonia knows nothing. Supposedly, she left because she panicked."

"Where was she?" Alex asked. "What happened? How did she let Gracie go?"

David shook his head. "She's of no help. She just let them take Gracie, then she panicked and did nothing."

"But, where is she?"

"What difference does it make? She went to some cousin in San Diego."

"She's our only lead at this point," Alex said. "Did they say Sonia told them about her friend from the park or the chicken?"

"Alex, stop asking questions. I don't care about Sonia. She fucking turned her back on Gracie and wasn't watching her, and—"

"David, they need to ask Sonia what happened."

"They did, and now they're saying she, most probably, had nothing to do with Gracie's abduction. She was scared, so she left. They checked out the information on her profile, and it was all legit."

"No," Alex said. "Someone knew Gracie and her special Chicken Love. That's why the person was dressed in a chicken costume. The person had to know. It wasn't a coincidence."

"If you're so smart, why don't you find her?" He collapsed into the chair.

"David, I have an idea."

"What is it?" he yelled, raw and agitated.

"Jon, come here please," she said.

David looked at her, impatiently, obviously wondering why she would summon Jon.

Alex fixed Jon's collar and kissed his forehead. "I need your help. Did Sonia ever play with her friend at the park? The one she met at the mall?"

"She's big, and big people don't play."

"Okay, did the lady from to park leave with Sonia?"

Jon shook his head. "The lady from the park was there with her baby carriage, but I don't know when she left 'cause I was waiting for the bunny to pick me."

"We have to find the woman from the park," Alex said. "She might have gotten a better look at the person who took Gracie, or she—"

Alex stared off into space and wondered: Who was this woman from the park? How was it Sonia had met this woman, supposedly another au pair, so quickly after having arrived? Since Jon said this woman was at the carousel, did this woman also leave the scene? And did she and Sonia leave together? Alex's imagination took her to a horrible, dark place where the possibilities were endless.

"Now, I've got a chicken and a wacked-out babysitter and a woman from the park. And they all disappeared." David started to sob.

CHAPTER 28

Even though it was Easter Sunday, the family liaison agreed it would be advantageous for Alex and David to do a press conference. The liaison told them more people would tune in, and, being Easter, it would be more poignant.

"Poignant," Alex had repeated when the liaison said it. She didn't want to be poignant or pitied; she wanted Gracie back, their Gracie.

Willing to do whatever it took, Alex and David drove to the Costa Mesa Police Station, the station that was closest to the mall; that was where they had set up the secondary center. The main information center was still at the mall.

Once they arrived at the police station, they were escorted to the entrance. Reporters were snapping pictures, sticking microphones in their faces, trying to tease something sensational from them, use their grief to tug at the hearts of their readers, viewers, listeners.

Alex walked with her head down, like the criminal she felt she was. David followed, slowly, broken, hoping for answers. They passed through the entryway where six empty chairs were lined against the window facing the reception desk behind which two officers sat.

The press conference was to be held in the meeting room, and the liaison insisted they check out the room beforehand. Alex and David agreed but didn't know why—until they walked in. There was a huge picture of Gracie propped up on the easel in front. They stopped, looked at the photo, and, as though momentarily paralyzed, they couldn't even take a breath. David started to cry softly, quietly.

Gracie looked adorable in her frilly white dress, the outfit she'd carefully selected for her kindergarten picture. There she was, smiling at everyone. Her eyes, though blue, not brown like the Mona Lisa, seemed to have the same peaceful, intense connect. And the way Gracie's flowing brown hair framed her face and then cascaded down her back made her look angelic, ethereal. But Gracie couldn't be peaceful now, not now, maybe not ever. Alex wiped a tear from her eye.

Now, Alex knew why their liaison had insisted they stop in the conference room beforehand. Seeing Gracie's picture propped up in front of a room that would soon be full of law enforcement officials and reporters would have been too much for them to have handled without being forewarned.

Alex hoped David was going to be able to speak. He had to. Maybe if he pleaded with the person who took Gracie, then maybe the abductor would . . . No. It was too horrific to think about what things the abductor could be doing.

The liaison escorted them to the tiny break room and told them to wait there while reporters filed into the conference room. They watched the screen in the break room and stared as every seat in the conference room filled. The energy in the room was feverish: reporters waiting expectantly to get a good story, one that was informational but, more importantly, emotionally charged.

"I'm Chief Duswalt of the Costa Mesa Police Department and with me today are Special Agent Mohan from the Los Angeles office of the FBI, Sheriff Gulen, Detective Diane DeRoche Parker, and Pat Walley of the Costa Mesa Fire Department."

Hoping one of them had the expertise, some special training, a guarded secret that would return Gracie, Alex studied the people standing on the podium. The incongruency of these powerful officials with the picture of an angelic Gracie in the background made her heart sink. It was so routine, sterile, but this was their little girl, their family, David's heart.

Chief Duswalt continued, "At four p.m. yesterday, our officers were dispatched to South Coast Plaza mall, 3333 Bristol, Costa Mesa, to the carousel in response to a call from mall security about a missing child. Upon arrival, we spoke to Alexandra Rose, the child's stepmother, who stated the child, six-year-old Gracie Cain, was missing."

Alex saw David's lips tighten, his arms move across his chest, and she could almost feel his fear, his wrath, his despair.

Chief Duswalt stopped and looked at the FBI agent who had been standing on the podium with him and moved closer to the microphone. Duswalt continued, "The case was activated by us, and, following the appropriate protocol, a command post was set up with a secondary post here at the Costa Mesa Police Department. We are maintaining the primary information center at the South Coast Plaza mall. Additional assets were requested from the FBI as well as the U.S. Marshals, the sheriff's department, and police officers from surrounding cities."

He turned to the FBI agent, as though to diffuse the lack of success, showing it was shared and not just on his shoulders. "Investigation has revealed a suspect dressed as a chicken . . ."

There were laughs.

Alex and David exchanged a look, both wondering how anything about this could evoke a laugh.

Chief Duswalt continued, "The suspect, a six-foot-tall individual who concealed his or her identity by dressing in a chicken costume, was seen taking the child from an Easter parade at the carousel area at the South Coast Plaza mall. Then the suspect went into the men's room; therefore, we're currently working under the assumption the person dressed in the chicken costume is male. We have that on the camera, but we have no footage of anyone exiting the men's room wearing a chicken costume. The costumed suspect was last seen going into the men's room at the South Coast Plaza mall without the child. We're working on the premise he passed the kidnapped child to another person before entering the men's room. However, we do not have any screen shots of an exchange on any of the surveillance cameras."

There were gasps from the audience. Alex knew this story, had gone over it a hundred times, but still it filled her with as much terror as the first time she'd heard the costumed chicken no longer had Gracie in his possession.

The chief motioned to silence the audience as he recapped: "As I stated, no one dressed in a chicken costume was seen exiting the men's room. There was, however, a person approximately six feet tall in a bunny costume whom we did see 'hopping' out of the restroom. The possible change of costume by the person who we believe initially may have taken the child is indicative of a planned kidnapping and escape."

Once again, the audience whispered to each other.

He quieted them. "There were numerous mall staff members dressed in the same bunny costume working the Easter Bunny photo area at the mall at that time. We have questioned each of these persons and have reason to believe none of these paid staff members used the men's washroom at the time the costumed chicken entered the men's room or a costumed bunny exited."

"This is sounding like the *Wizard of Oz*," David said under his breath, clearly not interested in being the subject of public amusement.

She tried to take his hand, certain he was recoiling not just at the loss of Gracie but at the recounting of the surreal events. The details heightened the absurdity of the events and seemed to reinforce the improbability of tracking the abductor.

In an unmodulated voice, Chief Duswalt explained, "Of course, the Amber Alert has been put into effect, and we're asking anyone who has seen the girl, or the suspect dressed in a costume, to contact the FBI tip hotline, the police department, the local county sheriff's department, or your local law enforcement."

Then Chief Duswalt almost wept. "I'm asking the suspect to release her. He can leave her at a hospital, a convenience store, anyplace. We just want to get her back safe. That's our primary concern."

"Fucking better be," David whispered to Alex.

"We have nothing further but will answer your questions, and then the parents want to speak."

Someone in the audience asked, "Can you give us any other details regarding the abduction site?"

Duswalt answered, "We cordoned off the carousel area and searched the entire area, but now we're deferring to the FBI." He then motioned to the FBI agent to step up to the other microphone.

The FBI agent said, "We cannot confirm seeing the suspect without a costume. We've found the babysitter, who was the last person with the child."

178

David looked at Alex but said nothing.

Another reporter asked, "What else are you doing to find Gracie?"

The FBI agent responded, "As stated, an Amber Alert has been set up, and we are receiving leads and following up on those. We've also brought the babysitter in for questioning."

Alex's heart pounded, wondering whether she and David had asked Sonia enough questions, the right questions, when they'd hired her. Would it have mattered if they'd asked more questions? What would they have asked to have prevented this? Were they too eager to entrust their children to a stranger?

Someone asked the chief, "What other agencies are involved in a search?"

"We're using air, the sheriff's department, the police department, the FBI in Los Angeles, and we have requested additional federal officer staffing from the U.S. Marshals Service. We have the command post set up at the police department here. This is not unique to what we do in any kidnapping."

"Any kidnapping?" David repeated. And she knew to him, to the entire family, this wasn't just any kidnapping.

"Do you have the exact time?" someone asked and continued to request details about timing.

Alex didn't hear the rest of the reporter's question, but she did know she and Eric had been gone for forty-five minutes. Yes, they'd left Gracie and Jon alone, alone with Sonia for almost an hour. *Why? Why did I do that?* she wondered now, now that it was too late.

The chief stepped closer to the microphone. "Yes. We have an approximate time placed at 3:30 p.m. to 4:00 p.m. Anyone who was near the carousel, please contact our office."

"How important is time?" a reporter asked.

"Critical. That's why we're having this conference. The more eyes we have looking for the child the better."

"How many are involved in this?" a reporter asked.

Chief Duswalt stated it would be the last question before he called the girl's parents up to say a few words. "We have forty investigators from the police department, we have FBI assistance, and we're pursuing every lead and using technology to locate Gracie. But there are more eyes in the public than police officers."

Someone yelled out, "What're your thoughts on this?"

The chief signaled David to come to the podium. "Here's Gracie's father."

David took Alex's hand and went up to the podium with her. He stood and looked at the audience. Then he leaned forward and gripped the mike.

Alex didn't know whether he'd be able to speak.

"Please," he begged, not just to the members of the press assembled in the room but the viewers, hopefully one viewer, the one who could return Gracie. "We're asking the abductor to release my little . . ." He stopped. "She's just six and scared. She needs her family. Please."

The FBI agent saw David was going to break down. He stepped up to the microphone. "If anything develops, we'll schedule another conference, which will be at the Chamber of Commerce."

David took the microphone again. He appeared determined, composed, ready to disperse everyone to find Gracie. "We're asking everyone who was anywhere near the carousel to come forward. And we're pleading with the abductor to just drop Gracie off, no questions asked. Please, if you ever loved anyone . . ."

CHAPTER 29

A lex and David left the police station and proceeded home. Although they decided to go ahead with the family Easter dinner, claiming it would help if the family was together, it was even more painful than they could've imagined. Everyone pretended it was a normal holiday celebration, but it wasn't. It couldn't be. Nothing would be normal again. Everyone was morose, careful not to mention Gracie's name.

But it was good to be with Meredith, Warren, and Cecile—people who felt the loss almost as much as David. Alex and the boys, actually, everyone was trying as hard as possible to be kind to each other, nicer than they'd ever been toward one another.

The only incident they had was when Meredith and Warren gave the boys their gifts.

Meredith reached into her Louis Vuitton satchel and took out the children's Easter gifts. She placed three navy blue boxes and one pink box onto the table. As she handed each boy his gift, they thanked her, but stared at the pink box remaining on the table.

"Open your gifts," Warren said, but he too looked at the pink box.

Eric opened his first—a Garmin Vivofit 3 GPS smartwatch. "Wow, this is perfect to track my workouts."

"But it's a smart watch," Daniel said, obviously taking a dig at Eric's proclivity for sports, sometimes at the expense of grades.

Jon opened his next—a teal LG Gizmo Gadget watch. "I can't tell time yet," he said.

"It's a tracker," Meredith said. "Can't be too cautious in this day and age." Then she covered her mouth, realizing this was the wrong, terribly wrong, thing to have said.

"I have one too." Cecile held up her wrist. "Guess they don't want to lose me either."

Solemnly, Warren pointed to the pink box on the table. "I bought them all two weeks ago, but I wanted to wait for Easter. If only . . ." He started to cry.

With uncharacteristic compassion toward Warren, David said, "No, the bastard would have taken it off."

"Only if he knew she had it," Alex said. "This could have..." She stopped. There was no reason to give David another "if only." He'd been tormenting himself with enough of those every minute since Gracie was abducted.

Then Daniel opened his gift, thanked them for the watch, and mentioned the FBI's new application called Child ID, which allows parents to store photos and information about their child, and then if something happens, the information is sent directly to law enforcement officials.

David had said it was too late for that. But when Alex reminded him Jon was still little and, in addition to the watch, it would be a good thing for him, David had gotten angry. He said, "How can you think of your children now? You'll never understand the loss of a child."

Softly, she'd said, "I do understand missing a child with all your heart." There was no need to remind him about the time she'd lost custody of her boys. This was different. It wasn't just a sense of loss; it was terror, raw terror.

Immediately after dinner, David retreated upstairs. Usually a great help in the kitchen, insisting since she cooked, he'd wash the dishes, now he didn't seem to care. He didn't seem to care if he ate, didn't seem to care if the dishes were done. Nothing mattered to him—except Gracie.

Alex and the boys cleaned up the dishes, talking about the meal as though it were an ordinary holiday dinner, but careful not to mention how much Gracie was missed, how beautiful she was, and how sad they all were.

Alex put Jon to bed, read him a story, and then kissed him on the forehead. "Good night, Cookie Face," she said, and started to leave his room. But before she left, she went over and checked the windows, making sure they were locked. Keeping the children safe had been something she'd taken for granted, something instinctive—until it wasn't, until she'd failed.

She walked down the hallway to the older boys' rooms. Reminding them not to stay up too late, she gently shut each of their bedroom doors. Then she passed Gracie's room. She walked in, but the silence was too much for her. She sat on the bed and cried. Guilt, fear, loss all grabbed her and wouldn't let go. As she looked around the room, pink, lavender and white—everything girly, frilly, she thought about Gracie. How far away from the softness of this room was she? And if she was even alive, was she being forced to do terrible things, things no little girl who should be asleep in her own bed with a pretty pink flowered comforter pulled up to her face should do?

Alex reached for Gracie's yellow Chicken Love, but it too was gone—at the police station being used for scent tracking, instead of comforting Gracie now, when she needed it the most.

She grabbed Gracie's pillow and inhaled. Now, it didn't matter that Gracie would dab a drop of Harper's perfume on herself before she went to sleep. Alex went over and opened the perfume bottle, letting the scent float through the room and understanding why Gracie needed the connection.

She closed the door to Gracie's room and went to her bedroom. David was sitting on the bed, staring into space. He looked at her. "I'm terrified about what could be happening to Gracie," he said.

"I don't want to imagine," she said. There were no words that could soothe his pain. That she knew. She also knew his loss was not only of the present; he had lost the possibility of a future. He was going to walk Gracie down the aisle at her wedding, hold her child, his grandchild, in his arms. Gracie was not only his daughter, she was his legacy.

Alex started to stroke his back.

He pulled away and took a breath as though he was preparing to say something but didn't.

She nodded. Any touch that wasn't Gracie, any connection, she was sure, felt like a betrayal. It wasn't fair that they were here safe while Gracie was out there possibly experiencing horrific, unimaginable things, things no six-year-old should ever know.

"Maybe if you talk about it," she said. "Then it might—"

"Okay, you want me to talk. I'll talk." He looked at her. "You . . ."

"David, why are you so angry with me?"

He grabbed her shoulders. "I went to the safety deposit box last week."

Confused, wondering why he'd care about anything in the safety deposit box and what significance it could have now, in the middle of this nightmare, she asked, "Why?"

"Gracie had been asking for her necklace, the one she wore at the wedding, the one Harper had when she was a little girl."

"David, what does this have to do with me?" She couldn't imagine he would suspect her of taking the child's necklace.

"Cecile wanted Gracie to wear the necklace on Easter, and—"

"Was it there?" she asked, worried it wasn't. Thinking that had to be the reason he was so upset, the only possible reason. But she couldn't imagine how it could have been missing from the vault since she and David were the only ones who were on the signature card and no one else had a key.

"Yes, the necklace was there." He glared at her.

"And?" she asked. This wasn't like him. True, he'd been agitated and volatile lately. That was completely understandable. He was obviously worrying whether he—whoever the "he" was—was feeding Gracie, whether he was raping her or worse. Had he sold her? No, she couldn't think about that. It was too terrifying. It made her whole body tighten, and she felt chilled.

David tightened his grip on her shoulders.

She pulled back. "If the necklace was there, what's the problem?"

"There's a very big problem." He shook her.

She was fearful of him, the man she thought she could trust, the man she thought was kind and gentle and would never hurt her. She could only imagine the pain he was in, but that didn't account for his anger, anger he was directing at her and everyone, for that matter.

"I reviewed our will," he said.

"What does that have to do with . . ." She stopped. The losses were too much for David. As strong as he appeared, Alex feared losing first Harper and now Gracie was too much for him to bear. "David, I'm here for you."

"You," he yelled. It was as though another person had invaded his body. He was angry, almost to the point of hysteria.

"What did I do?" she asked, her familiar insecurity and self-doubt flooding her. She believed she was responsible for losing Gracie.

"Alex, you stand to gain a lot of money if—"

"David, how could you even think I would stoop to such a cruel and horrific act?"

As though he didn't even hear her, he said, "You and Gracie get everything if something happens to me, and if Gracie's gone—"

"You're crazy!"

"Yes, I am, and so would you be if your child were missing, but maybe, just maybe—"

"How could you even suspect me of—"

"I suspect everyone, everyone!"

"David, I'm your wife."

His eyes were wide, filled with tears. "You have to tell me whether you're a part of this whole thing."

"David, I'd never—"

"Never what?" he yelled. "Lose my child at the mall?"

"I love Gracie. You're not the only one who is hurting, worried, scared."

He stood there, tears welling in his eyes. "Alex," he said, and started to hug her. Then he stopped and turned away.

As he left their bedroom, she called to him but knew he had to go to Gracie's room. She also knew that was the only place where he felt connected, hopeful.

CHAPTER 30

Unable to sleep after that horrific confrontation with David, Alex finally heard him return to bed at four. He was becoming more and more angry by the minute, and she understood, felt for him, knew she'd be experiencing the same emotions.

In the morning, when she tried to wake him for work, he lashed out at her. He asked whether she'd be able to work if one of her sons was missing. As she dressed for work, she felt guilty, guilty for trying to carry on a somewhat normal life when his had stopped. She asked if he wanted her to stay with him, but he told her he needed to be alone.

Fearful of what he might do if he received bad news while she was gone, she hesitated about going to work. Then she decided he would call if he received any information, anything. He'd told her she couldn't help anyway. She knew as hard as she tried, nothing short of Gracie would comfort him.

Rushing, she had to get to work on time because her patients had been scheduled back to back, and she needed to leave work early in order to take Daniel to his orthodontist appointment. She'd wanted to cancel the appointment, but Daniel begged her to keep it; he was so eager to have his braces removed.

While at work, she tried to concentrate on her patients. Their pain was what she had to think about, not her own. She left work early and rushed to pick up Daniel at school and take him to his appointment. She felt guilty going on with her life when David was paralyzed. Her mundane routines seemed an intrusion in their new life, a life that was focused on one thing and only one thing—finding Gracie.

Just as Daniel was taken back to the orthodontist's office, Alex had to go to the ladies' room. "I'll be back in two minutes. You go with the assistant."

Daniel followed the orthodontist's assistant back and then hesitated at the door. "I can't go into this room," he yelled, loudly, uncharacteristically.

Alex rushed out of the bathroom. "What's going on? Are you okay?"

Daniel ran into the waiting room, shaking.

Alex hugged her son. "What happened?"

"They had bunny ears on the chair," he said. "How could they do that to me?"

Dr. Licauco came out of one of the rooms and put her hand on Daniel's shoulder. "Let's go back. I promise this will be painless."

"That's not it." Daniel shook his head. "I can't look at bunny ears on the chair."

"It's Easter season, and I always cover the chairs with those bunny ear chair covers," Dr. Licauco said.

"Gracie, Gracie," Daniel repeated. "She was taken at the Easter parade. This makes me . . ."

Alex was surprised. Daniel hadn't talked about how he felt about Gracie's abduction. As a matter of fact, no one talked about it. It was as though only David was in pain, but in reality, the entire family was affected. Everyone was grieving, feeling the loss, trying to cope.

No, it definitely wasn't only David who was in pain. Alex had lost David; he was gone, only there in body. He was distant, lost, and those were his good moments. Other times his anger overtook him, and he'd lash out at Alex, obviously angry with her for what he called her carelessness. He'd blame her for leaving Gracie with Sonia for so long. Alex would try to defend herself, explaining Sonia was the nanny and Alex joining them was just a spur-of-the-moment decision. Gracie and Sonia were going to the mall anyway.

David would listen to her repeat the same story, insisting she go over every detail, certain in the retelling he'd find some clue, any clue.

"We can take off the chair covers," the orthodontic assistant offered.

"Okay," Daniel said. "That would be good."

He went back, ready to have his braces removed, and Alex followed to the room, which now was sanitized of Easter Bunny ears, any reminder of Gracie's abduction.

Daniel was the perfect patient, calm and cooperative.

As soon as they got in the car, Alex turned to him. "Why didn't you tell me how you felt about what happened to Gracie?"

"Mom, everyone was so worried about David. You kept telling us not to upset him, how bad he was hurting. You said we could never understand what it's like to lose a child. So, I didn't say anything."

"Daniel, you can always talk to me about anything."

And on the car ride home, they talked about Gracie. Alex told him her worst fears, and he confirmed the probability that the outcome wouldn't be good. He'd been reading day and night, compiling statistics and stories, hoping to find solace in them. And as though the numbers would prove Gracie was okay,

Daniel cited statistics confirming the chances of her return weren't good.

"Why?" Alex asked.

"Okay, listen to this: If there are 360,000 child abductions a year and fifty percent or 180,000 are taken by family members and the other half is almost equally divided between acquaintances and strangers, then only 90,000 are taken by strangers."

"Why is that good?" she asked. Unlike Daniel, she wasn't comforted by information; it made the loss of Gracie more real—a statistic.

"Mom, of the ninety thousand, most are taken for short periods and then returned, but . . ."

She took her eyes off the road for a second and looked at him. "Daniel, I'm so afraid."

"Me too, because there are approximately three hundred who are . . ."

"We have to hope," she said, just as they pulled into their driveway.

They walked into the house. It was so quiet, almost as though even Lucky knew not to bark. Alex patted Lucky.

David was home, sitting in his chair. She didn't want him to pick the other boys up from school; she knew seeing other happy children would have been too much for him to bear.

There was food on the dining room table, provided by, of course, her First Friday Book Club women. The boys sat down and helped themselves. Alex brought David's food to him in the family room, knowing how painful it would be for him to sit at the kitchen table and stare at Gracie's empty chair.

He left the food untouched. She took away the plate and gave him a protein shake, begging him to at least drink that.

At seven o'clock his phone rang.

No caller ID, definitely a burner phone, one of those prepaid phones which aren't traceable.

He answered it. "This is Doctor David Cain."

Alex went into the family room and stood, waiting, watching, fearing.

"Yes. Oh, God yes." David started to cry. He motioned to Alex to get him a pen.

"Anything," David said and wrote down some numbers. "By Thursday, but I need . . . Okay."

Alex held her breath. Her heart was pounding, and she was too terrified to be hopeful, but she wanted to be; she needed to be. "What did they say?"

"They have Gracie and want five million dollars wired to this account." He held out a piece of paper.

She took the paper. "Can we?"

He glared at her. "How can you even ask that? Of course."

"I'm not questioning anything. I wouldn't, but . . ."

"Alex, there are no buts. We will do anything and everything to get that money. I have to call my financial guy, and if I have to, I'll sell this house, my practice, anything."

"David, I'll sell everything too. I have my ring and . . ."

The policeman who'd been stationed in the van outside, listening to the call, came into the house. "We don't know if this is legit."

"I'm doing this," David said. "I want my Gracie."

"You need proof of life," the officer said.

David looked at the officer. "Proof of life? If it were your daughter . . ." He reached over and started to grab the officer's collar, but then stopped. "Do you have another plan?"

"No," the officer said. "But after they get the money, they often . . ."

191

Rage in his eyes, David turned to the officer. "If you guys know so much, why haven't you found Gracie?"

The officer explained when there was a kidnapping, they'd be able to track a Swiss or British account within hours, or, at most, a day; however, some offshore banks weren't always cooperative. The bank the kidnapper had chosen was in Mexico, so that might make it difficult to work with them. The police officer said they would immediately contact Interpol to get them to track the deposit.

"Do not interfere with this until my daughter is returned," David demanded.

"It's not up to you, sir."

"It's my daughter," David pleaded.

"We have to do our job," the officer said.

David glared at him. "If you intercede before I get her back—"

"Let me assure you, we've got highly trained—"

"Don't," David said, and went back to the family room without excusing himself.

Alex apologized for him, but the officer assured her David was reasonably calm considering.

CHAPTER 31

Tonight, even after the kidnapper's call, David was on edge. Finally, he fell asleep at midnight, only to bolt out of bed an hour later.

"What is it?" Alex asked.

David started to grab his shirt from the chair. "It's Warren."

She looked at him. Sure, he'd been crazed the past three days, but not like this. Now, he seemed possessed, angry. "What are you talking about? And why are you getting dressed?"

"I just figured it out. Harper gave Warren money all the time. Now that she's no longer here to give him money . . ."

She shook her head. "It can't be. Are you accusing Warren of taking Gracie? That's impossible." No, Warren's love for Gracie had been apparent the moment Alex saw them together, and Gracie idolized him. And according to David, after Harper's death, Warren had become more involved in Gracie's life than ever before. As hard as David tried to push him away, it seemed he tried even harder to stay close to Gracie.

"Gracie went with the chicken. It was Warren dressed as a chicken."

"David, you probably had a dream. Try to go back to sleep."

"Who else would have known she loved her Chicken Love? Warren knew that was Gracie's favorite animal, the one Harper had given her the Easter before she died."

She was uncertain as to whom to believe: David, who had a vendetta against Warren for supposedly wanting to take Harper to Mexico for an infusion, or Warren, who'd tried to give his sister some hope. "That's a little far-fetched," Alex said, but she suspected it might not be.

"Far-fetched?" he yelled. "If your child were missing, nothing would be far-fetched."

"Meredith would never let him do that to you, to us, to—"

"You and your First Friday . . . Maybe, just maybe it was Meredith who masterminded the whole thing. Meredith with all of her fancy jewelry and her . . . You think you can trust every-one, but believe me, you'd trust no one if—"

"Please think about what you're accusing him of. How would he have known Gracie was going to be at the mall?"

Like a caged animal, waiting to get at his prey, David said, "Gracie talks to Warren at least twice a day."

"But Gracie wouldn't have known what time we were going to the mall."

He looked at her like she was the enemy. "I know what my gut is telling me," he yelled, and started to leave the bedroom. "When Harper died, I always thought Warren . . ."

"David, you said that before."

"Like I told you, I had no proof. I couldn't chance Gracie losing her grandmother. And it wouldn't have brought Harper back anyway, but now . . ."

She knew David was raw, angry, scared. He was lashing out at everyone. First, he'd accused her of leaving Gracie on purpose, standing to gain from her abduction. He'd apologized for that, admitting he was crazed and grasping at anything, but now . . .

"Alex, I just told you, Warren kept taking money from Harper, but now, since that's no longer possible, he needs money. I know . . . I'm going to confront him."

Alex didn't blame him for accusing everyone. If anything happened to one of her children, she'd be crazed too. She ran after him and told him to wait. "I'm going with you, but first let me go upstairs and wake Eric, tell him we have to leave."

"Alex, you don't have to come with me."

"I'm driving," she said. "You're too upset."

"Upset. That's a mild word. I'm not upset; I'm crazed. These have been the most horrific three days of my life."

She took the keys, and they got in the car.

The police car that was parked in front of their house pulled out as well.

"Why the hell are they following us?" David asked. "Why aren't they searching for Gracie?"

She looked over at him. "Daniel said the police suspect everyone, especially family members."

"If they're so smart, have them find her!"

Since the freeways were empty at two in the morning, they arrived at Meredith and Warren's house in the canyon within twenty minutes. So unlike the home Harper built, this house was spacious, but shoddy. Meredith and Warren were living there temporarily—and they made that very clear—only until they found one that better suited them.

"Do you want me to sit in the car and wait?" she asked.

"No, I need you," he said, and rang the doorbell.

Meredith answered. "Do you have news about . . . ?"

195

Alex stared at her. She'd never seen her without her perfectly coiffed hair, perfectly applied makeup, and . . . She chastised herself for even thinking such thoughts when Gracie was in danger and now, when David was going to confront, but hopefully not accost, Warren.

David rushed past Meredith. "I need to talk to Warren," he shouted. "Get him down here now."

"Warren," Meredith called up.

David screamed: "You took her. I'm searching this house."

As Warren walked downstairs, he said, "David, calm down, I—"

David started to lunge at him. "Don't tell me to calm down. My daughter's missing."

Warren leaned away. "How could you even think I'd take her? For what? For money? I don't need your money."

"Oh, yeah," David yelled. "You've been taking it for years. Now, you're hiding Gracie—"

"I'd never stoop to anything that low." Warren looked at David.

Alex and Meredith sat down on the sofa. Alex was fearful about what David was capable of. He'd turned into a different man, the loss of his child unleashing all of the secrets he'd kept buried. Now, it seemed he had no reason to hold anything back. It was almost as though without Gracie, he'd lost his will to live. Nothing seemed to matter.

"You've taken my Gracie like you took my Harper," David screamed.

Warren shook his head. "Like I told you before, Harper couldn't take the pain. She knew you'd pump her up with morphine. She wanted to believe the Laetrile would work. She didn't want to be kept comfortable, waiting for—"

"What's wrong with that?" David yelled. "And where were you taking her? There was a suitcase packed and—"

"That was when she gave up. I was taking her to Mexico." Warren started to cry. "It was her last hope; she believed she could get an infusion. She begged me to help her."

David went for Warren's neck. "My wife. She was my wife, you—"

Warren put his hand on David's arm. "It's not what it seems."

"Talk and talk fast. I don't know why I didn't go to the police when I thought you did it. I couldn't destroy all of Gracie's world, but now you've gone beyond even your lowest—"

"When Harper couldn't even get out of bed to go to Mexico, she decided I had to help her end it." Warren brushed away a tear. "I couldn't turn my back on her. She was going to do it anyway and didn't want to be alone."

"What about all the other money she gave you through the years?" David yelled.

"She never gave me any money," Warren insisted.

"I have proof," David yelled.

Warren shook his head. "Harper was being blackmailed and... I can't go on with this."

"You better . . ."

"Seven years ago, Harper met me for a drink at The Quiet Woman bar one night when you were away with those Flying Samaritans in Mexico. There was this guy at the bar, and . . ."

David glared at him.

"Listen," Warren said. "You were gone all the time. She'd been trying to get pregnant, as you well know. Well, it happened."

"No," David yelled.

Alex watched in disbelief. No, the man in the locket wasn't a one-night stand; he couldn't have been. If he were, then there would never have been a locket. No, there definitely was more to it. Warren was probably trying to make David feel better about his wife's infidelity. But this man meant more to Harper than a one-night stand; no one kept a locket hidden for a one-night stand. No, Harper was—or had been—tied to this man. Then maybe he changed, but there was a time when she probably was torn between him and David.

Warren wasn't telling the truth, but it was better that way. There was no need to make David hate Harper or Harper's memory. Yes, it was much better this way.

"I need to hear exactly what happened," David demanded.

Warren nodded. "He got into drugs. Then he started to threaten her, stating he was going to call you, and—"

"I don't care about him. Tell me, did she do a paternity test?"

"Yes," Warren whispered.

"Oh my God." David collapsed into the overstuffed black chair and wept.

Alex tensed. Then, at the same time, she and Meredith moved away from each other on the sofa. Alex suspected Meredith had known all this but didn't tell her. No matter how much the First Friday Book Club professed loyalty, the women were still loyal to their husbands first. That was true, definitely true, as David stood here accusing Warren of one horrific act after another, first of murdering his sister for a hundred thousand dollars and now of kidnapping Gracie for five million.

David looked up at Warren. "Tell me everything," he pleaded.

"Harper kept giving this guy money, and he promised never to contact you or Gracie, not that he had any interest in seeing his daughter."

"Don't say *his daughter*. Gracie's mine," David cried out. "Now, they're both gone. Gracie's gone. What did you do?"

"I loved my sister, and I love Gracie. I'd never do anything to that girl. She's like my daughter."

"Warren, why didn't you tell me?"

"I couldn't. Harper made me promise."

David wiped away a tear with the back of his hand. "No. It's not true. Harper would have had an abortion if—"

"David, you know she'd never have an abortion. She felt she'd already sinned by being unfaithful; it was a horrible indiscretion. But she feared if she had an abortion after all the miscarriages, there was the possibility she might never conceive again. Also, being a Catholic, she considered an abortion a mortal sin."

"A mortal sin," David repeated.

"But," Warren said softly, as though trying to make David's pain go away, "Harper and I decided, if you ever questioned the money, we'd tell you I needed money for gambling debts, anything. But she didn't want you to know."

Suddenly, David jumped up from the chair, ran over to Warren, and screamed. "That's the man who took Gracie."

"No," Warren said, his eyes darting back and forth as though he was processing something.

As Alex watched him, she wondered whether he was holding something back or if he was telling the truth. She just couldn't read him.

David glared at Warren. "If this man was blackmailing Harper, then he's the one who took Gracie. What the hell is wrong with you? Why didn't you tell me or go to the police?"

Without waiting for Warren to answer, David reached for him and shouted, "He has my Gracie. We have to find him."

Alex went to David and tried to put a steadying hand on his back, but he pulled away. Nothing was going to stop him now that they had a lead, their first real lead in this horrific nightmare.

"No," Warren repeated.

David let out a wail of pain, loss, and fear, fear that Gracie was harmed. "If that bastard didn't care enough to see Gracie, his own daughter, before, then—"

Warren shook his head. "But—"

"Take me to him," David screamed. "Now!"

"David," Alex whispered. She feared for David. He couldn't just go to a kidnapper's home without the police. He would put himself in great danger. But she also knew she'd do the same if one of her children was taken.

Patience long gone, gone after Gracie was taken, David screamed at Warren, "Why didn't you tell us about him? Speak!"

"He's dead," Warren whispered.

David glared at Warren as though he didn't know whether to believe him, as though he didn't know what to believe anymore.

Alex knew this emotional roller coaster was too much even for him. She turned to Warren and asked, "How do you know he's . . . Who is he?"

Warren looked back and forth at them, as though he was searching for an answer, something that would stop this endless questioning, each question apparently becoming more and more difficult to answer. "Thurston Brunner," he finally said.

Meredith gasped, her eyes widened, and her face started to flush.

David noticed it and turned to Meredith. "You. Why that reaction? Talk!"

Meredith fidgeted with a few strands of her long black mane. "I have no idea."

Alex saw Warren give Meredith a look. She wondered whether it could have been a look of caution or something else, something . . . "What the hell's going on here?" Alex asked.

Warren nodded. "Well, Thurston was a developer, and he had some big money trouble. His buildings were upside down, and . . ."

"How do you know all this?" Alex asked. Sure, the timeline was accurate; Thurston could have had a tryst with Harper—or more—and he could have fathered Gracie, but . . . She looked at Warren and waited. He seemed to be hesitating. Maybe because this was so difficult to reveal or maybe because it wasn't the truth.

"I . . ." Warren stammered and then stopped.

Alex stared at David. His whole world was collapsing right before him. First his beloved—yes, he thought she was his beloved—wife died, and then his daughter was abducted.

Suddenly, Warren seemed to compose himself and said, "Thurston kept threatening to tell you, so Harper would give him money. Every time, she thought one more time and then he'd stop. But he never did until . . ." Warren glared at Meredith as though cautioning her. "Until Thurston committed suicide."

"How would you know that?" David asked.

"Everyone knew Thurston," Warren said. "He held himself out as a pillar of the community; at every charity event he gave money, Harper's money, to every cause. He's lucky I didn't kill him myself."

"Warren, if that's true, how could you have let me hate you, think you were low enough to keep taking money from Harper?"

"I'd do anything to protect my sister," Warren said. "She didn't want you to ever know about Gracie's real father."

"Don't ever say that," David screamed. "I'm Gracie's father!"

Alex looked at her husband, a broken man. Tears welled up in her eyes and a lump rose in her chest. Everyone David loved was taken from him, a mirage. His marriage a sham—Harper wasn't the wife she'd appeared to be, and his daughter wasn't even his.

CHAPTER 32

On the car ride home, David told Alex he didn't believe Warren; he couldn't. Gracie had to be his daughter, but David couldn't have, wouldn't have loved Gracie more even if she was his daughter. No, she was his. She had to be.

But Alex suspected there was more, more about that man who was supposedly Gracie's father, to have caused Meredith, the perennially cool and calm Meredith, to become flustered.

Exhausted as she was when they arrived home, while David sat by the phone waiting for any further ransom instructions, she went to the computer and punched in "Thurston Brunner."

A philanthropist, that's what they called him; married, two children, an attorney, a developer . . . nothing extraordinary. She searched the projects that bore his name. His high-rise condominiums were mostly in Nevada, a very volatile market for sure.

She read on: Thurston's obituary contained salient facts about his life: forty-eight, husband of Cynthia (Cindy) Brunner, nee Winston, father of Tiffany and Tara, graduate of New York University School of Law . . . but there was nothing about him that would . . . Except his picture. He wasn't the man in the locket!

Alex stopped and called Meredith.

202

"What do you know about this Thurston Brunner?" she shouted.

"Alex, we're asleep. You can't just come over in the middle of the night and then call an hour later. I have work, and . . ."

"Work," Alex screamed. "Gracie's gone and you're thinking about work?"

"You went to work, if I recall," Meredith snapped.

Alex needed answers. "Meredith, you seemed to know who this Thurston Brunner is. The way you reacted when Warren mentioned his name . . ."

"I was shocked. I mean . . . Thurston Brunner, Gracie's father?"

Alex turned back to the computer and stared at the obituary. No, she'd never seen or heard of him before. "You say his name like we should all know him, but—"

"No, I was surprised Warren had never told me he knew Thurston."

"Why should he have if he promised his sister he'd never tell anyone?"

"But—" Meredith said.

"Tell me," Alex implored her.

"I clerked in Thurston's law firm, and . . ." She covered the phone.

"What is it?" Alex asked.

"Warren," Meredith said. "He's calling out for Gracie again. Since she's been gone, I hear him wake up and call out. He's distraught over Gracie. I've never seen him this anxious, ever. You know, he loves that girl, and if anything happens to her, I don't know what he'll do. Gotta go to him."

Alex hung up and got into bed, but she couldn't sleep.

Then at exactly six o'clock, David's cell phone rang. Once again, a burner phone. The picture on the screen was clear. There she was—his Gracie. Yes, she was his Gracie and nothing, not even Warren's horrific revelation, could change that.

"Daddy." That was all she said, and the phone cut off.

That was all he needed to hear. Alex knew he was going to liquidate anything and everything he owned even though the police and liaison had told him it didn't mean she'd be returned. They'd actually advised him against paying, stating that in these types of cases, the payment didn't guarantee the return of the child, and often, once the money was received . . . No, she couldn't think of those possibilities. She had to be hopeful for David, but . . .

After he heard Gracie's voice, he told Alex his daughter might never hold his hand again, but he'd always hold her in his heart. And he was going to do whatever was asked of him to get her back.

Then they waited.

Each passing day without a word from the kidnapper was torture. There were no new leads, but, in a sense, that was good. Maybe it meant Gracie was still alive.

Alex kept asking Meredith why Warren had never told her about the connection, but Meredith maintained it was Harper's secret, a secret Warren had sworn to keep. And, Meredith explained, since Thurston died way before Gracie was abducted, there was no connection. Alex didn't think it made sense, but she couldn't go to the police with this crazy story. It would just take them off their track.

◆◆◆

As instructed, David made the wire transfer to a bank in Mexico. Then, two days later, the call came.

A muffled voice greeted David.

"Yes," David said, the terror in his voice echoing throughout the room.

The phone was on speaker. "Your daughter is at the Center for Performing Arts. Pick her up now."

"Alex," David yelled, joy, relief, trepidation all resonating in his voice.

They started toward the garage. The police officer who was in the van across the street, wiretapping their phone, rushed in and told them to wait. "You have to go in a police car."

"No way," David said. "I'm leaving, and you better not fuck this up."

"It's protocol, and—"

"You've done nothing but tell me about protocol and acronyms since this started."

The police officer continued, "I called over to the theater. *Peter Rabbit* is—"

"Are you fucking kidding?" David screamed. "You're talking about Peter Rabbit and—"

"Sir, I was telling you intermission is just about over, and everyone is being ushered back to their seats at the performance of *Peter Rabbit*."

"There better not be any police." David ran to his car, and Alex followed.

"Sorry," the officer called to David's back.

When they got in the car, David turned to Alex. "Call the police and tell them if they dare to show up, I'll—"

"David," she said softly. "I think the police have to go in first. I mean, lots of lives could be in danger."

The man whose passion was rescuing children who'd been trafficked, the man whose practice was devoted to delivering healthy babies to their mothers, the man who flew to Mexico and other underdeveloped countries to dedicate himself to helping those who couldn't afford medical care now only cared about saving Gracie.

"Alex, I'm only concerned about getting my Gracie girl back."

"I know," she said. "But don't let her undergo the rape test."

Annoyed, he quickly glanced at her. "Why not? We've got to find this psychopath and make him pay for what he did to my child."

"They don't always send out the rape kits for processing," she said, but didn't want to tell him that the negligence in testing was part of the reason men like the one who took Gracie were out there. As a matter of fact, California Senate Bill 3118, addressing the issue of the unprocessed rape kits which were building up at police stations, just passed. And she'd heard an interview with Mariska Hargitay, the founder of the Joyful Heart Foundation, which advocates for timely processing of rape kits. Ms. Hargitay estimated there were over 13,000 kits in police stations which were unprocessed. And an investigation found three California police stations which had failed to process over fifty percent of the rape kits. The senate bill would require a state-wide audit of untested rape kits. No wonder, up until now—and she hoped it would be only up until now—there were so many evil people, people who preyed on innocent girls and did things she hoped hadn't happened to Gracie.

He pulled up to the theater.

Lights flashing, four police cars were already lined up in front of the theater, and then three more police cars and a fire engine rushed to the scene.

Several officers surrounded the usher who was holding Gracie's hand.

David jumped out of the car and ran to Gracie.

"I love you," David said, his words almost trite compared to the emotion Alex knew he had to be feeling. He looked at Gracie as though she was a sunrise, and in a sense, she was—his sunrise. Tears of joy streamed down his face.

They were ushered into a police car. This time, David agreed. As long as he had his Gracie girl, he didn't care where they took them. Gracie clung to David and let him put her in the police car. A police officer assured Alex they'd drive her car to the station. Alex gave the officer the keys and joined Gracie and David in the police car.

"Daddy, I was scared." Gracie started to cry. "The lady left me at *Peter Rabbit* all by myself."

"Who?" Alex breathed a sigh of relief. If the person she was with was cruel to her, then Gracie wouldn't have said she was scared when the woman left the theater. Or, Alex was afraid to think, maybe they'd brainwashed her or had done something... "Who?" she repeated.

"The lady from the park—Sonia's friend." Gracie sniffled.

Shocked, Alex looked at David. Now, Alex's suspicions about Sonia were heightened. Could she have executed the kidnapping or was she in any way connected to the abductors? It made no sense.

David called to the officer in front. "You have to go and pick up Sonia. She knows who took Gracie," David said as he stroked Gracie's hair, the long brown locks shorn, her beautiful hair bleached out and blonde. "Where did they take you?" he asked, and Alex knew he feared the answer.

Gracie looked up at him. "Daddy, they told me I had to stay in my own room—alone. When we went to the car, they put a bandage on my eyes, and the man said if I didn't play their game and tried to take it off, they'd hurt me, bad."

"Did they hurt you?" Alex asked, heart pounding, terrified of the answer, but needing to know and sure David couldn't bring himself to ask. But he wanted to know, needed to know if his baby had been harmed.

"No, only when I cried for you, Daddy. I even cried for Jon 'cause he's my favorite of the boys." Gracie looked at Alex. "And you, too."

Alex wiped a tear from her cheek and then from Gracie's. She pulled her close and hugged her. "I love our Gracie girl."

Tentatively, David asked, "Who hurt you when you cried?"

"The lady was the mean one, and . . ."

David sighed.

Alex knew women could also do horrific things to children and so, she knew, did he.

Gracie grabbed on to her father. "The lady cut off all my hair and changed it to yellow, just like my Chicken Love."

"You're still my beautiful Gracie girl."

Gracie sobbed. "I cried, and I couldn't understand what the lady was saying, 'cause she would talk in Sonia's language. I was so scared of her 'cause I think she told me I'd never be Gracie again if I wasn't good. And . . ."

"What?" David was holding back tears.

"I wanted to come home, but the lady told me they'd only take me home if I behaved."

The police officer drove them toward Hoag Hospital.

"I don't want to be here," Gracie said between tears. "I need to see my grandma Cecile and my uncle Warren." Then she started to sob so hard she couldn't even speak. "I . . . I . . . miss them."

The police car pulled up to the building adjacent to the hospital where the physicians' offices were located. David was going to protest but didn't.

Alex knew he wanted to, needed to, know exactly what had happened to Gracie. "Remember, don't let them use the r-a-p-e kit on her," she whispered.

208

Gracie looked terrified. "Why are you spelling? Is something else that's bad going to happen?"

"Nothing bad will ever happen to you again," David said, and gave Alex a cautionary look.

The officer said, "We'll get her examined here, and then we'll go to the station. We'll need to rush on the interrogation, so we at least have something to go on."

Heart pounding, fearing the worst, Alex followed them to the doctor's office. The doctor welcomed them and then said the mother could come into the room while he examined Gracie, but it was best that the father waits outside.

"I don't have a mother." Gracie whimpered.

The doctor looked at Alex.

"I'm the stepmom, but my husband can go in the room. He's a doctor."

"Any parent can be in the room," the doctor said.

"I'm not leaving my daughter alone," David said, as though he didn't hear the physician.

Alex knew he was about to say "again" or "with her," but he didn't. He just followed the doctor into the room, carrying Gracie. Alex waited outside while the physician did a gynecological examination.

When David and Gracie came out, David whispered to Alex, "No indication of physical abuse."

"Thank God," Alex said, at least one fear abated.

David told her the physician had checked Gracie for bruises and cuts as well as under her nails. He also took some scrapings, but it didn't appear there was any violence, any mistreatment.

Alex laughed at that—as though kidnapping wasn't mistreatment.

They went back to the police car and proceeded to the Costa Mesa Police Station, all the while Gracie begging to go home and see her "whole family."

Sergeant Cindy Matalucci, an attractive blonde-haired woman with warm brown eyes, introduced herself and walked them back to the conference room at the station. Gracie looked at the picture of herself, blown up on an easel, and started to cry. "That's not me anymore."

True, her long brown hair had been chopped off and her shorn hair was bleached, but she was Gracie, their Gracie.

"We need to know everything that happened to you," Sergeant Matalucci said.

"I told my daddy I couldn't see. They told me if I took off my eye bandage thing, then they would make me blind or do more than cut my hair off. I was scared of them."

"She was blindfolded," David said.

"Sir, please let her answer," the sergeant said.

"She's six." David stroked Gracie's hair again.

Alex looked at David and thought maybe touching Gracie's short hair made him feel more secure, reassured that was the only part of her they'd hurt. But she knew it wasn't true. It would take a long time for Gracie to recover. It wasn't only physical trauma that could damage people—that she knew too well. She touched the scar on her right wrist.

"What about when you ate? Did you see the place?" Matalucci asked.

"They told me I had to eat in my room," Gracie said. "I missed everybody. I was so scared, and I cried. A lot."

David was ready to walk out. "I don't see where this is getting anywhere except torturing my daughter with all this talk about what she ate, and—"

"No, Daddy, I hated the food. She was a bad cook."

Matalucci turned to Gracie. "What about the bathroom, Gracie? Did you go out of your room and see things outside?"

"No, they put a potty in my room like a baby." Gracie started to cry. "The lady came in and took it out. It was like a baby, but I'm not a baby."

Sergeant Matalucci continued to ask questions.

Alex held her breath as she waited for Gracie to answer. Gracie explained she didn't see the man because her eyes were bandaged. She said he was sometimes nice and would come into her room and . . .

David gasped. "Did he hurt you?"

"He told me stories. Then I think I heard the lady telling him not to go into my room, but he said this was his only time to see me. Then . . ."

Alex wanted to ask Gracie about the man who'd said that to her. Why, she wondered, would he have said that? Maybe that was a lead, but then she heard David plead with the sergeant. "Do we have to do this? She needs to go home and . . ."

The sergeant said, "We need as much information as possible. Gracie, please continue."

Gracie climbed on her father's lap. "The man would tell me stories, stories he made up. He even told me a story about a girl whose mother was dead, and—"

Alex looked at David. "How could he have known that?"

"Sonia probably told the lady in the park," David said. "Who knows what Sonia and the woman talked about instead of watching Gracie."

The sergeant nodded in agreement. "We questioned Sonia numerous times, and she insisted the lady in the park was just another au pair. She didn't know much about her. Sonia said she was from Mexico and they only talked about the families they were working for, and that was all. They'd just met two weeks before, and they'd agreed to go to the mall together for the Easter parade."

"See?" David said. "She knew all about us from Sonia."

"No, I'm not sure that was how it happened," Alex said.

CHAPTER 33

W hen Alex and David walked into the house, Gracie was so frightened that she clung to her father, even when Lucky nuzzled her.

"We love you," Jon said, and handed her a brand-new Chicken Love which he'd bought with his own money. When the police had refused to release Gracie's beloved Chicken Love, he'd insisted Alex take him to the toy store, and he bought a new stuffed animal to put on Gracie's bed for when she returned. At that time, Alex had hoped it wasn't futile, but she had to do it, had to hope.

Eric stood next to Gracie and awkwardly welcomed her back. "Glad you're home." He patted her back.

Daniel walked up to Gracie and hugged her. There were tears in his eyes. "We missed our Gracie girl so much." He kissed the top of her head, obviously being careful not to say anything about her shorn long brown hair.

Gracie reached out for the new Chicken Love tentatively, then grabbed it and held it close.

Everyone was careful, careful not to ask her any questions about what had happened or where she'd been. It didn't matter; all that mattered was that they were a family again. Even setting a plate of mac and cheese down in front of Gracie's chair was cause for celebration.

They quietly spent the next few days trying to adjust. Since Cecile could no longer drive, Alex would pick her up almost every day, understanding how much Gracie needed her. Gracie and Cecile spent most of the time upstairs, closeted away from the family, quietly playing with the tea set, reading books, painting their nails, doing whatever it took to distract Gracie during the day.

It was the nighttime that was the worst. David would stay in Gracie's room until she fell asleep. Alex would hear her crying, whimpering, and David would run to her, promise her it would never happen again; he'd always protect her.

◆◆◆

Three weeks later, Alex overheard Gracie in the family room asking David, "But if the man isn't in the jail, can't he come back for me?"

"The police will find him soon," David said.

"Daddy, why didn't the police catch the bad man?"

Alex also wondered why it was taking them so long. She walked into the family room and asked, "Gracie girl, tell me about the man who took you to the house for a little while."

Gracie shook her head. "Like I keep telling everyone, I was so scared."

Alex stroked Gracie's short blonde hair with the brown roots just starting to grow in, a reminder of the horrific thing that had happened just three weeks ago, a memory that would never leave her, never, ever. "I know, sweetie, but can you remember anything about him?"

"I don't want to remember."

But with each day that passed, it seemed the police were further and further away from finding Gracie's abductor. The bank in San Miguel de Allende, Mexico, to which the money was wired, had finally agreed to cooperate and assured them they just needed a few more days to release the information on the person to whom the money had been wired.

David looked like he'd aged several years, and even the slightest noise or ringing of his cell would make him jump. He could no longer maintain his gynecological practice and had applied for a job reviewing medical charts—something he could do from his home office. As a matter of fact, he never left the house—without Gracie. He was scared, actually terrified. He became even more committed to Child Rescue and spent every minute he wasn't with Gracie working on fundraising for the organization. After seeing firsthand how changed Gracie was, the Child Rescue creed, "Every child deserves a childhood," became more than a motto; it became a mantra, his mantra.

After a lengthy interview and background check, Alex had hired a college student to transport the boys. She was too fearful about asking David to leave his vigil watching over Gracie, so she cut down on her office hours.

Usually, Alex would rush to work, see her patients, and then return home, worried that something would have or could have happened in her absence. Now, three weeks after Gracie's abduction—yes, for them, life was divided into before the abduction and after—life was starting to return to normal, a new normal.

So, when Liz called and insisted Alex join the First Friday Book Club for their May meeting, Alex initially protested but then agreed. This group was her lifeline, and only death or a catastrophic event such as this one—yes, Gracie's abduction was catastrophic—could prevent the women from attending the meetings.

Today, Alex's last patient before lunch had canceled, so she arrived before any of the other women. She took a seat and opened *Sunburn* by Laura Lippman, this month's novel.

Liz waved to her from the entryway and made her way to the table.

They exchanged hugs, and Liz sat down next to her. "How's Gracie?"

"She's doing a little better during the day, but it seems her nightmares are getting worse." True, there were periods of time, very brief periods, when she was fine, but then she would become hysterical for no reason. Well, in truth, she had reason—every reason.

Liz twirled her long pearl necklace and looked concerned. "Is the psychologist helping at all?"

"The psychologist says it will take time, lots of time, and Gracie keeps asking when they are going to put the bad people in jail, but . . ."

"I bet David keeps asking the same," Liz said.

"It's so frightening," Alex said. "That's why I'm going to sell my practice."

"Alex, it's such a shame you have to give up your career for his child. I mean . . ."

"No, it's for the boys too. After this, I don't want to work so far away from the children."

Liz motioned to the waitress, who came over to fill their water glasses just as Terrie and Meredith started toward their table.

"Look how striking she is." Alex pointed to both of them, but Liz knew she was referring to Meredith, who today looked especially elegant in her stark white Chanel suit, white blouse, and a long, thin diamond necklace. She did look like a model, a high-fashion model.

Waving the April edition of Oprah's magazine, Meredith rushed to the table. "We're trendsetters! Oprah actually recommended *Sunburn* this month."

Terrie, clad in her usual, a peasant blouse and flowing floral skirt that went to her midcalf, leaned over and hugged Alex before taking her seat. Terrie had told David he could call her anytime, and he did. Before he'd selected the child psychologist for Gracie, he'd turned to Terrie for the referral. Terrie was more than helpful and assured him Gracie would be fine, but it would take time, lots of time, just like the psychologist told them.

Judi rushed to the table. "Sorry, late as usual."

The waitress came over to take their orders: Chinese chicken salad for everyone except Terrie, who was back to her hamburger and fries.

Liz reached for the magazine. "Well, I guess having the main character kill her husband in cold blood is the way to get Oprah to notice a book?"

Judi tapped her glass with her long red fingernail, her marquis diamond ring glistening. "Could you even fathom killing your husband?"

"My former husband—absolutely," Alex said, and took the magazine from Liz.

"The main character was clever, very clever. I loved her diabolical plan to get custody of her daughters," Meredith said.

"You loved her?" Alex asked. "What about the man who took Gracie; he had a diabolical plan too. Did you love his plan?" And before Meredith could answer, she asked, "Did you think he was clever too?"

"Alex, it's a novel," Meredith reminded her. "I'm not talking about reality."

"Sorry," Alex said, but it was reality for her. The police, the FBI, no one was even close to finding the abductor, and Gracie was terrified. They all were.

Liz twirled her pearls and tried to relieve the tension, divert the conversation to *Sunburn*. "Killing her first husband with a knife and . . ."

Terrie shuddered. "But in the end, she got to make a life with her two daughters."

"Being able to live with your children is a blessing so many take for granted," Alex said. She knew what it was like to walk into a child's empty room and wish for the sound of them laughing, talking, even bickering. After Gracie's return, Alex felt thankful, grateful.

The waitress delivered their lunch.

Without waiting for the others to start, Terrie picked up her thick hamburger. "In my practice, I see how impressionable children are."

Meredith shrugged. "I, for one, never could understand why you all want to have them around. I mean, it's so nice with Gracie—take her for the day and return her." Meredith took out her cell phone and showed her screen saver with the picture of her, Warren, and Gracie. Then she swiped forward to a picture of the new home she and Warren were in the process of purchasing. "Is this *moi?*"

Alex gasped.

The women looked at her.

She said, "I was just thinking about . . . Nothing." But she was thinking about Warren, Warren and Meredith who were supposedly so devastated, and yet it seemed they'd put an offer on the house during Gracie's kidnapping.

No, Alex decided, they had to have found the house before the abduction, but the timing was not making sense. Maybe, just maybe, Meredith made him put in an offer on the property while Gracie was gone. Maybe Warren was so distraught he left everything to Meredith. And maybe they had to move quickly on a property like that, a three-million-dollar property.

"Warren said he has to live near Gracie," Meredith said, calling Alex back to the conversation.

"Sorry, I was thinking of something." Alex looked at Meredith and took a breath. Yes, she'd been thinking about how similar Meredith was to the main character in the novel *Sunburn*. They both could be cold, calculating—without a conscience if it benefited them. She looked at the photo Meredith had been holding. "Your new house is amazing."

Terrie wiped some ketchup from her chin. "I miss having you near me, though. First you moved to Warren's house in the canyon and then—"

"Warren's house wasn't me. I mean, no ocean view. This," she said, "is *moi*."

Terrie laughed. "Meredith, do you remember when you lived in Irvine, next door to me, before Warren? What ocean were you seeing in Irvine?"

Meredith pursed her lips. "Trade up."

"Yes," Judi said. "And speaking about trading up, next month we're scheduled to read *The Dirty Book Club* by Lisi Harrison, a *New York Times* bestselling author."

"It's fabulous," Terri said. "I already read it and loved it."

Alex pushed her plate away. "Since we've had so many dirty secrets, maybe the First Friday Book Club should be changed to the Dirty Book Club!"

CHAPTER 34

Unlike any Mother's Day before, this day promised to be special, although fragile, especially for Gracie. It had been over three weeks since she'd returned home, and she still was terrified of anything that wasn't forewarned, predictable. Even normal household routines were fraught with a fear that was tangible.

Alex went to join David, Gracie, and Jon in the family room. Gracie looked up at David, who nodded and winked. Then Gracie went to the drawer where they kept the picture albums and took out an envelope. She handed the pink envelope to Alex. "For you."

Alex took the envelope and kissed Gracie's forehead. As she opened the envelope, her heart started to pound. The words *To My Mother* printed across the card shocked her. She turned to David, who smiled at her, and then to Gracie, who puffed out her chest and struck her self-satisfied pose. As Alex read the loving words on the inside of the card, signed *Gracie*, a tear fell onto her cheek. She was beyond grateful, and swooped Gracie up and kissed her. "Thank you."

"Daddy said it would be okay to call you Mommy. So, is it?"

Jon looked up from his Lego set and stared at Alex, who knew he wasn't going to be happy with her response.

"Absolutely, 'cause I love our Gracie girl." Alex put Gracie down. "Now, let's go up and get dressed for our company."

"It's not company." Gracie put her hands on her hips. "It's my grandma and Uncle Warren." Then she scrunched up her nose. "Oh, and Auntie Meredith, who isn't fun but wears the best lipstick and always lets me try it on."

David looked over at Alex and shook his head. "No lipstick for my little girl."

"Daddy, Auntie Meredith lets me," Gracie said.

"Let's go upstairs," Alex repeated. "Everyone will be here soon."

"Yeah," Gracie said. "My best family's coming!"

Jon walked up to Gracie and shook his head. "I thought we were your best family?"

"Yes, but you're not the whole family." Gracie turned to her father. "Right?"

David nodded. "Yes, Uncle Warren and Grandma Cecile are your family too."

"Told you," Gracie said, and followed Alex upstairs.

Alex helped Gracie put on her pink Easter dress, the dress they'd picked out together, the dress she hadn't gotten to wear on Easter. Then Alex started to comb Gracie's hair. Actually, it still wasn't long enough to braid, but Gracie insisted she needed her braids back.

Alex smiled at Gracie. "I love your Easter dress."

"I didn't get to wear it on Easter," Gracie said. Then she looked at Alex. "If the man who took me isn't in the jail, will he come back for me?"

"The police will find him soon," Alex promised.

Gracie buried her face in Alex's skirt and started to cry. "But why didn't the police catch the bad man?"

Alex, and all the boys for that matter, tried to do whatever they could to help Gracie forget her horrible ordeal, especially since the police weren't any closer to finding the abductors.

They did have photos of the woman who'd left the theater and matched those to the mall photo of the woman Sonia identified as Luz; however, when they tried facial recognition, there was no match to a passport. Absolutely nothing matched the facial recognition database.

◆ ◆ ◆

Suddenly, the doorbell rang, and Alex heard David greet Meredith.

"Where's Warren?" David asked.

As soon as Gracie heard Warren's name, she started toward the door. "Uncle Warren's here!"

Alex followed Gracie downstairs and greeted Meredith. When Alex hugged Meredith, she felt her tense up. "Is something wrong?" Alex asked.

"Oh, no," Meredith replied. "Warren's probably picking up Cecile."

"Probably?" Alex asked, and then motioned to Gracie to give Meredith a kiss.

Gracie shook her head.

"Gracie girl." David picked her up, whispered something in her ear.

He put her down, and she went over and looked up at Meredith. "Happy Mother's Day, Auntie Meredith, 'cause even though you have no kids, you've got two cats, and you're their mommy."

Obviously uninterested, Meredith said, "Cute," as she reluctantly bent down to receive a kiss.

David motioned to Gracie and said, "Let's go outside to take a picture of you in your beautiful, um, dress."

Alex knew he'd almost said, "Easter dress," but stopped himself, certain any reference to that horrific Easter, the Easter where her beautiful pink dress was thrown into a big black plastic bag and taken to the police department for scent recognition, was too painful for him to even think about. Alex knew for David, every one of Gracie's hugs, every kiss was something he might never have had. Now, there was an intensity to each and every moment with his little girl. Now, even the smallest touch was sacred.

As soon as David and Gracie left the room, Meredith whispered, "I don't know where Warren is."

"What?" Alex asked.

Meredith started to cry.

"Did you have a fight?" Alex asked, certain that was the only possible reason Meredith didn't know where he was. They were both volatile and probably fought over some stupid thing, and Warren left. But she wondered why he wouldn't have returned by now, especially since he was supposed to bring his mother over for a special Mother's Day lunch.

Meredith shook her head. "No, as a matter of fact, we were having a nice day."

"Well, what's the issue?"

"I had a migraine."

"And?" Alex knew how debilitating migraines could be, causing someone to crave a dark room, no sound, no smells, just a cold cloth and sleep, and sometimes they'd last for days.

"I took an Imitrex and went to lie down at about four yesterday afternoon. I must have fallen asleep right away 'cause I didn't get up until midnight and then fell back to sleep."

"Wasn't Warren in bed?"

"He sleeps in the guest room whenever I have a migraine."

"But do you have any idea when he left?"

"This morning, I was in bed, waiting for him to bring me breakfast. I mean, I thought, since it was Mother's Day, he must have been downstairs making breakfast for me, and . . ."

Alex soothingly rubbed Meredith's arm. It was clear Meredith was distraught. Gone was her self-confident reference to herself as *moi*. Meredith Blackstone was sad and troubled.

Meredith blotted her eyes. "So, I waited. When he didn't come to my bedroom, I went downstairs and found this note from him." She reached in her purse and read the note. "Darling, I ran out to meet the jeweler to pick up your Mother's Day bracelet and a little something for my mom. Be back in a while."

Alex took the note and looked at it as though that would make any more sense. "Meredith, he could have just gone to get the jewelry and then—"

Meredith held out her cell phone for Alex to see the call log. "I called him eight times, but it just kept going to voice mail."

"Did you call Cecile?"

Meredith shrugged. "Of course, but she's such a ditz. She doesn't know what's going on half the time anyway."

"Meredith, she has Alzheimer's. What do you expect? And what time did you see the note?"

"Alex, I told you, this morning when I went downstairs."

"Why didn't you call the police if you discovered he was missing?"

Meredith looked annoyed, impatient. "You don't call the police when you think your husband is at a jewelry store."

"When do you think he left?" Alex asked.

Meredith took a deep breath. "I went to his room, but I couldn't tell if he'd slept in his bed . . ."

224

"His room?" Alex repeated.

Meredith sobbed. "What the fuck? Truth is, he has his own room. No, I, Meredith Blackstone, the one who keeps telling everyone the secret to a good marriage is sex, haven't had sex with my husband since Gracie was gone. He hasn't touched me. I thought it was just this devastation about her, but then when she came back, he continued to be distant, agitated. Every little thing stressed him out. I couldn't even talk to him. Finally, yesterday, he seemed calmer, like he'd made some peace with it."

Shocked, Alex thought about Meredith sleeping in her own bedroom, about the things that appeared real—like love and sex—but weren't. No, she shouldn't judge. Each couple created the relationship that worked for them—until it didn't. And Meredith's was no exception.

"Are you really sure he wasn't home last night?" Alex asked.

"I told you his bed was made, but he always makes it." She sobbed. "Why are we talking about making beds?"

She knew Meredith was embarrassed about confessing her sex life wasn't as she professed.

David came back into the house and walked past them on his way to the kitchen. "Cecile just called, and she wants to know if someone's coming for her. I'm going to pick her up."

"I wanna go too," Gracie said. Ever since she'd come back home, she clung to David even more than before. She wouldn't let him out of her sight. She refused to go into her own room unless someone went in before her and turned on the light. But the psychologist said Gracie was doing very well, considering the circumstances. The psychologist said she was doing so well because she had such strong support from her family. He'd also told them how important it was for Gracie to see her grandmother as much as possible. And of course, there was her favorite, Uncle Warren, the one person in her extended family whom the psychologist insisted was the strongest link to her mother.

Meredith's phone rang, and she reached over to answer it. "Warren?" she said, without looking at the phone number.

Alex watched Meredith's face turn ashen.

CHAPTER 35

Meredith, perennially cool, calm Meredith, shouted into the phone, "What the hell happened? Tell me, now."

"Why's my auntie crying?" Gracie asked.

"I have no idea." Alex pulled Gracie to her lap and stroked her hair. She feared something terrible had happened or was about to happen, which she hoped wouldn't invade Gracie's already precarious world.

Meredith hung up and said, "Warren's dead. I know it."

"No," Gracie yelled at Meredith. "Daddy told me only my mommy died, and everyone else will always be here with me."

David picked up Gracie and started to carry her outside with him, but she wriggled out of his arms. "I need Uncle Warren." She started to cry.

"What's going on?" Eric came downstairs and walked into the family room with Daniel close behind.

Alex motioned for them to go back upstairs.

Meredith could barely speak. "Warren," she repeated. "The police," Meredith choked out, "went to our house," she said between sobs.

Alex and Meredith went into the living room. Always dramatic but usually composed, Meredith couldn't stop crying and gasping for air. She was so unsteady that she almost collapsed as Alex helped her to the couch.

"Tell me what's going on," Alex said softly.

"The police!" Meredith shouted.

Gracie ran into the room. "Do they have the man who won't take little girls ever again?"

"Get her out of here," Meredith barked. "This isn't funny."

Alex got up and walked Gracie back to the family room. "Gracie girl, we need to have a big-people conversation," she said, and then returned to the living room.

"Sorry," Meredith said. "I didn't mean to yell at her."

"Tell me what happened."

"The police said they came to the house looking for me," Meredith repeated, her voice thin and weak and her body trembling. "They're coming here to take me to the station. Me!"

"What happened to Warren?" Alex asked.

"Warren?" Meredith screamed. "The police wouldn't tell me what the hell was going on, but they said something absurd about a gun that was registered to Warren, and—"

"Warren has a gun?" Alex was shocked.

"First time I heard of it, but I guess there's a lot about him I didn't know."

"Maybe someone stole his gun?"

"Alex, how naïve are you?" Meredith started to weep. "I'm sorry," she said as she crumpled into Alex's arms.

As Alex held Meredith, she felt her relax a little, just a little.

Suddenly, Meredith pulled away and looked at her watch. "They'll be here soon. They said they needed me to identify something. It's not good."

"Do you think something happened to Warren?" Alex asked.

At the mention of Warren's name, Gracie once again started to enter the room but stopped.

Alex shook her head and put her finger on her lips.

Gracie turned and went back to her dad, probably sensing something was amiss. Yes, now Gracie seemed to have developed a sixth sense, a caution that she'd never had before. Gone was her sense of adventure, gone was her daring everyone to do things; in a sense Gracie was gone . . . again.

Alex jumped when the doorbell rang.

When she opened the door, the shorter of the two police officers asked, "Meredith Blackstone?"

Alex stepped outside and closed the door behind her. She couldn't risk Gracie seeing police officers in their house. Alex was certain if Gracie saw the police in her house, it would frighten her.

After talking to the policemen, Alex returned to the living room and summoned Meredith, who went outside with the police officers.

A few minutes later, Meredith walked in, vacillating between abject horror and anger. "They're taking me to the police station," she sobbed. "And I need you to follow."

As Alex followed the police car to the Rialto station, she kept thinking about Meredith. There was something in Meredith that she'd never seen before. Meredith actually seemed nervous, afraid. But Alex didn't know if she could really read Meredith. Like the main character in the novel *Sunburn,* Meredith, brilliant and calculating, was capable of ruthlessness, especially when there was something she wanted. And Meredith wanted that house, that three-million-dollar house. Maybe, Alex thought, just maybe, Gracie's abduction could have been Meredith's idea. But then she decided Warren would never have been involved in anything that would have brought harm to Gracie, his Gracie girl.

And Meredith probably loved Warren. She wouldn't have been with him unless she got something out of the relationship. She always took care of herself just like she always tried to convince the First Friday Book Club women to do the same, professing the importance of self-preservation, self-care, self-everything. That was Meredith's mantra, her *moi*.

◆◆◆

The Rialto Police Station was weathered: the wooden reception desk was chipped, and the aqua Formica countertop was peeling. Alex walked up to the desk and explained to the officer she was here with Meredith Blackstone, the woman who'd been called in to identify certain personal effects.

The desk officer stared at Alex for a moment. Then he picked up the phone and announced, "I've got a lady here who says she's Meredith Blackstone's friend." Then he looked up and told Alex they would take her back for questioning.

"Questioning?" Alex repeated.

"Yes," the desk officer said. "Officer Brauning is going to be right here. He'll take you back to ask you a few questions because you know Ms. Blackstone."

"Me?" Alex was shocked. Why would they want to talk to her? There had to be something going on, but it was probably between Meredith and Warren. Maybe Meredith hadn't told her the truth about Warren not being home. Alex didn't know what to think.

Officer Matt Brauning, a handsome man with piercing blue eyes, came up to the front and escorted Alex back to a small office with a desk and two chairs. He sat behind the desk and motioned to the two chairs facing his desk.

Alex surveyed the soil-covered chairs. She decided on the faded blue chair for absolutely no reason. She sat down and looked at the officer.

Officer Brauning said, "You're here because you're a friend of Meredith Blackstone. That makes you a person of interest in this case."

"Case?" Alex asked. Her heart started to pound.

The officer asked if she knew about the explosion last night in Rialto, at the meth lab.

"We heard about it on the news," Alex said, and then explained, "But we shut the TV off as soon as we heard something about a baby dying." She tried to recall the details of the explosion last night. They didn't want to upset Gracie, and there wasn't any reason to turn the TV back on—there was nothing that concerned them, or so they thought. Now, here she was being interrogated about that very explosion in the meth lab in Rialto, and she was a "person of interest" in the case, the case that didn't involve her.

Then Officer Tanya Targett, a striking blonde who looked to be about thirty-five, came into the room and stood by the door.

Officer Brauning asked Alex question after question. He asked about her relationship to Meredith and Warren: how well she thought she knew them, how often she saw them, what she thought about their relationship, and other questions, questions she answered about the Meredith and Warren she thought she knew.

Then Officer Brauning swiveled his chair to the side where the computer screen was located. He clicked on a picture and turned the screen toward Alex. "Do you recognize this man?"

Alex stared at the screen. She gasped as she looked at Warren, Warren with half his face blown off. She thought she would faint. "Yes," she whispered. "Warren."

Then the officer forwarded to another picture. "Have you ever seen him before?"

Alex stared into the eyes of the man in the locket. Her chest tightened, and she started to sweat. *What could the man in the locket have to do with Warren? What could anything have to do with the explosion in Rialto?*

The officers glanced at each other, registering her reaction. Officer Brauning spoke first. "You know him?"

"No," Alex said. In truth, she didn't know him.

"You seemed to react. Is there something you can tell us?"

"No," Alex repeated. She couldn't tell them she'd found his picture in a locket, a locket that belonged to Harper. And, in truth, there was nothing she knew about him. "Who is he?" she asked.

"The woman who lived in the house with him was out walking her dog at the time of the explosion, so she was unharmed. She identified his body: Shaun Duvall. Does that name sound familiar?"

Alex shook her head. No, the name wasn't familiar—only the face.

The police officer continued, "This Shaun Duvall was a renter in the house, the house where the meth explosion was, and . . ."

Her heart was pounding, and she could barely breathe. "What does any of this have to do with Meredith and Warren?" But she knew it must have had everything to do with them. Why else would she be sitting here and staring, first at the grotesque photo of Warren and then at this man, the man whose picture was in the locket?

Officer Brauning nodded at Officer Targett, who then left the room. Then Brauning said, "We've identified a gun registered to a Warren Pearson, Meredith Blackstone's husband. That gun was fired, and that's what we think set off the explosion, and . . ."

Alex watched as Officer Brauning flipped to another picture on his screen. Alex had no idea what anything meant. *This is spinning out of control*, she thought as she stared into the screen. It was the woman who was in a few frames at the mall, the woman Sonia had met in the park, the woman who'd invited Sonia and Gracie to the Easter parade at the mall. "Do you know this woman?"

"I think so," Alex said. "Who is she?"

"That's what we're asking you," the officer said.

"I . . ." Alex said. She almost gasped for breath; the room was stuffy, and, once again, she thought she'd faint. "I think," she said, trying to regain her composure, "that was the woman who was at the carousel at the Easter parade when our Gracie was taken."

"We know all about the kidnapping," the officer said, his voice suddenly softer, his empathy apparent. "Do you know this woman?"

"I told you," Alex said. "I saw her picture on the computer screen at the mall."

Officer Brauning nodded. "As I said, she lived in the house. She was the mother of the fourteen-month-old who died in the explosion. Survived only because she had to walk her dog. Ironic. And, no driver's license, no passport, barely speaks English."

Officer Targett came back. "We're working on the texts," she said, and placed a plastic bag on the desk.

Officer Brauning looked at the contents of the bag and asked Alex if she recognized the bracelet.

Alex leaned forward, touched the bracelet, the one Warren always wore. The gold links were charred, but the gold bar in the center was intact. Alex turned over the plastic bag and saw the inscription: "Harper, 4/12/76 – 6/14/16." Yes, Warren loved his sister, but did he love money more? Alex looked at the bracelet and wondered whether a person could ever know another person, what he truly wanted and what he was capable of doing to get it.

"Can you tell us why Warren was at a meth lab?" The officer folded his arms across his chest, obviously hardened to death.

"No." Alex shook her head.

CHAPTER 36

Looking as though she'd aged ten years, Meredith had black mascara running down her cheeks, and red and swollen eyes. She appeared frail and weak, too weak to even stand. She crumpled into the empty chair next to Alex and sobbed.

Alex put her arm around her.

Composure restored, if only for a fleeting second, Meredith wiped some of the mascara from her cheek and demanded, "Let's get out of here."

Just then Sergeant Sabatino, the one who'd been interviewing Meredith in the other room, walked in and turned to her. "We need you back for more questioning. Some more evidence came in."

"I'm sitting right here." Meredith folded her arms across her chest.

The sergeant said, "We've been reviewing the messages on Mr. Duvall's phone. The girlfriend or whoever she is gave us the access codes, and there were texts between Duvall and Warren Pearson."

"I'm telling you, my husband was not an addict," Meredith shouted, each word louder and angrier than the one before.

Alex turned to Meredith and said, "I'm sure that'll be established." Then she looked at Officer Brauning for confirmation. "Right?" Alex knew how concerned Meredith always was about anything that would tarnish her carefully guarded image, besmirch her character, but she genuinely looked grief stricken.

Sergeant Sabatino continued, "As I stated, we were able to retrieve a few texts from Mr. Duvall's phone about a meeting last night around the time of the explosion." The sergeant looked at Meredith, as though reading her for information. "The texts between Mr. Duvall and your husband—"

"And what's that supposed to mean? My husband went there and set the place on fire?" Meredith shook her head. "This is preposterous."

"Well," the sergeant said, "it seems your husband was certain there was a SWIFT number and—"

Prone to drama, usually able to take control of a situation, Meredith appeared shocked, genuinely shocked. "What the hell is a SWIFT number?"

"It stands for Society for Worldwide Interbank Financial Telecommunications, and it's how we refer to the routing number from an international bank. Once money is deposited, the bank proceeds with the transfer," Sabatino said.

"No," Meredith yelled at the sergeant. "Warren never got any money. He kept telling me he had this deal that was going to fund." She shook her head. "But it didn't; Warren was terrified our house would fall out of escrow, and . . ."

"Some Mexican banks don't always release money to the recipients," the sergeant said.

"Good to know," Meredith said, obviously seething but grasping on to her caustic humor, trying to appear strong, unflappable.

Sergeant Sabatino nodded. "It seems your husband knew the money was wired and instructed Duvall not to harm the other girl."

Meredith gasped. "Has to have been just a text error." She had a look of sheer horror. "And now you're alleging my husband went to this meth addict's home, and . . ."

"My question, Ms. Blackstone, is, did your husband ever travel to San Miguel de Allende?"

"Where's that?" Meredith asked.

"Mexico," Officer Targett said.

Meredith recoiled as though trying to push away everything, everything that had thrust her into this nightmare. "We'd never go to such a backward, third-world country. We did go to Acapulco for Christmas vacation, but it was to a luxurious resort."

Targett nodded. "Well, the money was wired there, but the bank didn't release the funds to the recipient."

"Can they do that?" Alex asked. It wasn't her place to ask questions. She wasn't really involved at this point. But she was. Gracie, their Gracie, was the pawn in this horrific plot.

"Mexican banks can do whatever they want," Sergeant Sabatino said. "We suspect there was an altercation between Duvall and your husband over the money, and . . ."

Meredith had a look of sheer horror. "And now you're alleging my husband went to this meth addict to get money?"

"We think your husband could have fired the gun," the sergeant said. "Duvall would never have fired a gun."

Meredith's eyes widened, and she looked at the sergeant. "And now you're saying this guy, this lowlife, would never fire a gun?"

"Yes," Sabatino said. "Duvall would have known. Meth labs are highly explosive, and—"

"Also good to know," Meredith said with bravado, bravado Alex knew she didn't have at this moment.

"So, it was your husband who—"

"Now my husband is the one who caused the fire?" Meredith folded her arms across her chest. "He's dead. And I refuse to assume responsibility for the lives of some stupid drug dealer and his family. I have arrangements to make, and I'm sure you understand my grief." Meredith got up and walked out of the room.

As Alex watched her leave, broken and sad, she also realized Gracie's beloved uncle Warren had to have masterminded the abduction. That was why they'd put in an offer to purchase that outrageously expensive home right after Gracie was abducted. Yes, Warren had been living off of Harper his whole life and couldn't find another way to sustain his lifestyle.

Then Alex thought Warren could never do that, but she knew, she really knew it had to be true. She wondered whether you could ever really know another—or trust for that matter. Warren, wonderful Uncle Warren, was evil. And Gracie's real father was beyond evil.

No. She stopped herself. David was as real a father as any girl could want. "This will destroy Gracie. Warren was her beloved uncle." Alex started to cry.

Officer Targett sat down in the chair next to Alex. "Let me call BACA, and . . ."

"BACA?" Alex repeated, and started to phone David but stopped. This was something she had to tell him in person, something beyond even his suspicion about Warren's part in Harper's death.

"BACA is Bikers Against Child Abuse," Officer Targett said and started to dial. Then Alex heard her speak to someone and explain the third body had just been identified. She explained the guy was Gracie's uncle—yes, that Gracie, the beautiful little girl everyone knew, the girl who was abducted and then returned.

As Alex listened, she tried to imagine how they were going to tell Gracie that, besides her father and her grandma, the only other person she loved in the world was gone, gone like Gracie almost had been.

"Alex," Officer Targett said softly, calling her back.

Alex started to cry, not for Warren but for Gracie.

"We're going to help you. After you tell Gracie, BACA will be there."

Alex walked to her car.

Arms folded across her chest, Meredith was standing there waiting for her.

They drove for fifteen minutes, neither one speaking until Alex finally asked, "Why?"

"Gracie wasn't supposed to be hurt," Meredith said.

"You knew?" Alex was shocked, absolutely shocked. Yes, Meredith was beyond narcissistic, a trait they all recognized and accepted. But this was sadistic. "How could you?"

Meredith wiped some mascara off her cheek and blotted her eye. "Warren did it for me."

Alex was livid; she felt her heart pound, her chest tighten, and she thought she was going to swerve off the road. She turned and looked at Meredith. "You and your fancy jewelry and that new house. Why, Meredith? Why would you hurt an innocent child whom you supposedly love?"

As Alex drove, she waited for Meredith's response, but really, there was nothing Meredith could say to justify what Warren did, what she did, what they did together.

Meredith touched Alex's arm and sobbed. "Gracie wasn't supposed to be harmed or . . ."

Almost losing her grip on the steering wheel, Alex pulled her arm away. "Are you crazy?" she screamed. "Being abducted will scar her for life."

"Warren did it for me," Meredith repeated.

"Meredith, you said that, and I'll never forgive you for . . ."

Barely above a whisper, Meredith said, "Warren thought Duvall also took my daughter, so Warren . . ."

"Your daughter?" Alex again almost veered off the road. Wondering what child Meredith could be referring to, she reminded her, "Meredith, you hate children."

Meredith sniffled. "I was jealous. My daughter . . ."

"You have a child?" Alex asked incredulously. She wondered how anyone could have a child and never . . . No, that was Meredith; there was always something amiss whenever they'd talk about children—some disdain that seemed so unusual, defensive, suspect.

"Jealousy," Meredith repeated and sobbed. "Warren thought Duvall took my daughter."

"He took Gracie. What are you talking about?" Alex asked, certain Meredith's grief over Warren was causing her to babble incoherently.

"The night Harper met Duvall, I was there at The Quiet Woman. That's when I met Warren."

Alex was getting impatient. Gracie was abducted, Warren was dead, and Meredith was talking about how Harper met Duvall. It was making no sense. "What does that have to do with anything?" Alex shouted, but she feared it had everything to do with the nightmare, the terrible nightmare of Gracie's abduction.

"Duvall was teasing me about drinking while I was pregnant, and . . ."

Alex quickly looked at Meredith. "You were pregnant?"

"I told him it wasn't my baby, so I didn't really care." Meredith laughed. "But as it turned out, I really cared. I followed her every step, every milestone, I . . ."

Completely confused, at a loss, and trying to comprehend what Meredith was saying, Alex asked. "What are you even talking about?"

Meredith reached for a tissue. "I was a law clerk at Thurston Brunner's firm."

"You told me that before," Alex said.

"I had no money. I was poor, dirt poor."

"Meredith, I thought your father was some oil guy in the Midwest."

Meredith shook her head. "He was white trash. When my mother died, he drank, couldn't hold a job, and brought home one woman after another. He would beat us if we so much as said a word while the women were in the house. I had huge debt—college, which he didn't want me to go to, and then I went to law school."

"What does this have to do with Gracie?"

"Thurston was so nice to me, and he . . ."

"Thurston?" Alex repeated. "You had his child?"

Meredith shook her head. "Well, in a way. He knew how much debt I had, and his wife couldn't become pregnant. They were looking for a surrogate. Sixty thousand dollars, that's what they paid."

Alex gasped. "You had a child for money?" Meredith definitely was even more mercenary than Alex had ever imagined. But, maybe in a sense it was an act of generosity for both.

"So, after I delivered, it was so hard to give her up. I'd actually fallen in love with the little . . . Tara, Tara Brunner. I was supposed to have been her Auntie Mere. You know, 'Mere' is French for mother. But, Thurston's wife didn't really want me to have contact with her."

"I'm sorry," Alex said. She genuinely was sorry for Meredith. Any mother who loses her child, even a child she only knew for a few moments or hours, longs for her child forever. But, Alex wondered aloud, "What does this have to do with Gracie."

Meredith continued, as though she'd waited all her life, or part thereof, to tell her secret to someone—the burden of holding it was too great. "Shortly after I gave up the baby, Harper became pregnant."

241

"But how did you know Gracie wasn't David's child?" Alex asked, shocked to her core at the secrets people keep to protect others, but really in the end they destroy us.

"Alex," Meredith said. "Harper would never tell me. Sure, I knew she was seeing this Duvall. When David was out of town, the four of us would go out: Harper, Duvall, Warren, and me. We became the Four Musketeers. It was so much fun, but once she became pregnant, she was like Mother Teresa: no alcohol, early to bed, nothing exciting. I think Duvall knew the baby was his because he was so protective, but . . ."

"No," Alex said in disbelief. "Was Harper going to leave David?"

Meredith grabbed the wheel. "Watch where you're going. You almost got us killed. Killed. All dead." Then she laughed. It wasn't a joyous laugh; it was a laugh of hysteria as though this was too much for even cool, calculating Meredith to handle. She continued to laugh.

Alex pulled over onto the shoulder, stopped the car and turned toward Meredith. "This isn't funny."

"Nothing is funny," Meredith said, "especially now. Nothing . . ."

"Was Harper going to leave David?" Alex repeated.

Meredith stopped laughing and a tear fell down her cheek. "She'd never leave David. She loved him. The whole Duvall thing was just loneliness. Once she had her baby, she wanted nothing to do with him. He was crushed. He wanted her, and then that's when it happened."

"What?"

"Duvall got into drugs. He was a wreck . . ."

Alex handed Meredith another tissue. "But how would you have known about Duvall possibly taking your child too?"

"Duvall was Warren's friend then, and he needed money. He'd been doing contracting for Warren, but then he just fell apart. He couldn't keep a job."

Alex had gotten so involved in Meredith's story about Harper, she forgot about the other baby, Meredith's baby. "But what about you? Your baby?"

"I'd made what I thought was an easy deal—get inseminated, carry the child, and then goodbye, done, but it wasn't like that. I loved my little Tara. After I gave her up, I had trouble listening to Harper. All she talked about was Gracie. I was devastated, and she was glowing. Then Warren was smitten, and all he talked about was his Gracie. I broke up with him, threw myself into my career. It became my child—a child no one could take away."

Alex nodded. She'd done that when she'd lost custody of her children. Yes, she'd tried to make her practice fill the deep emptiness; but it couldn't. She reached over and put her arm around Meredith. "But you and Warren got back together, and . . ."

"Yes, we were trying to have a baby, but Gracie was his first love. I knew that, and . . ."

"Meredith, I'm so sorry." Alex was sorry, sorry for the secrets we all keep, the secrets that burn a hole in our hearts and make us bitter. "But why would he have let Duvall do that— take Gracie?"

"Duvall was evil. He threatened to do more if Warren didn't agree to his plan." She sobbed. "When Warren refused to do it, Duvall told him he was going to take Gracie and sell her to a trafficking ring if Warren wouldn't go along with his plot."

Alex started to cry tears of relief that Gracie hadn't been trafficked. "Duvall wouldn't have done that," she said, but really, she had no idea what someone who could turn his back on his daughter was capable of doing to his child.

"Alex, you really are naïve. Of course Duvall would have. All he cared about was money and getting back at Harper for . . ."

"Harper's dead," Alex reminded her.

"And now, so is Warren!" Meredith sobbed. "And Warren went to Duvall's house for me."

"Meredith, I still don't get why Warren was at Duvall's."

Meredith tried to compose herself. She pulled down the mirror and looked at her mascara-smeared face. Then she turned to Alex. "That abduction that was in the news last week, Tara Brunner. My Tara."

"I didn't really follow it, but . . . oh . . . Thurston's daughter . . . wow." In truth, Alex had turned off the car radio when she heard about it, and at home, they rarely ever listened to news anymore. Sure, she'd heard about it, but she'd just thought Thurston's family was cursed, unlucky—first he kills himself and now his daughter's abducted. At first, she'd thought it was a copycat of Gracie, since Thurston had been known to be very wealthy, but then there was no ransom request, so it wasn't the same as Gracie's abduction.

Meredith was sobbing again. "I know Warren suspected Duvall had taken her. I'm sure he went there because he thought she was there. He didn't tell me he was going, but I know that's what he thought. Why else would he have gone there?"

If that's what Meredith needed to believe, then Alex wasn't going to destroy her with the possible truth. The possibility that Warren was evil and did everything for money still lurked in Alex's heart. But it didn't matter now. Warren was dead, Duvall was dead, and Gracie was scarred for life.

"I'm sorry," Alex said. "But after Gracie, we're . . ."

Meredith sobbed. "Everything isn't about Gracie. I'm hurting, hurting to the bone."

Alex got back on the road and for the remaining hour of the drive home, they were silent—each one holding on to their newly acquired information, information that proved how greed could make you do things you'd never fathom yourself capable of.

As soon as they got home, Alex parked.

Meredith rushed to her car and sped away.

CHAPTER 37

A lex walked into the family room and stopped. Heart racing, she stared at the television. There on the screen, staring back at her, was a photo of Gracie. The reporter was explaining how Gracie, the Gracie who was abducted just a few weeks ago, was related to the man who died in the meth lab explosion last night.

"Where's Gracie?" Alex asked.

"She's upstairs with Cecile having a tea party for Chicken Love's birthday," David said, just as Gracie walked into the room clutching her Chicken Love.

David grabbed the remote and clicked off the TV. But it was too late, way too late.

Gracie stared at the screen. Yes, she'd seen both the photo of herself and that of Shaun Duvall right before David had been able to click off the TV.

David reached out to her, but she turned her back and ran to the corner of the room to her red toy box with the little jewels around the edge. She dug through the box, throwing her American Girl doll onto the floor, then her little kitchen set, pots and pans clanking all over. Then she grabbed her pink sequined purse, the one where she kept her jewelry. She flung her purse onto the coffee table and opened it. She reached into her purse and pulled out a locket.

David looked surprised. "What's that and who gave it to you?"

Gracie looked at Alex. Obviously embarrassed about having gone into Alex's jewelry box, she said, "My mommy always let me look at her pretty things. And it has a picture of Mommy, my beautiful mommy."

"But . . ." Alex was going to say it belonged to her, but it didn't. Harper had carefully hidden it in the shoe box, with the Christian Louboutin red shoes, the shoes that fit Alex perfectly.

David put his arms around Gracie, trying to reassure her, trying to erase the photo of her on the TV screen. He must have felt her heart racing because he said, "Gracie girl, everything will be fine."

Trembling, Gracie asked, "Why were they showing me on the TV with the man in the locket with Mommy?" But before they could answer her, make her feel safe, Gracie asked, "Is he going to come get me? And did he make my mommy leave me?"

Alex kneeled down, opened the locket, and looked Gracie in the eye. "Is this the man who took you?"

"I told you, the lady put bandages on my eyes so I couldn't see when the man came into my room, and . . ."

Even though Gracie had said the man didn't harm her, and the examination confirmed that, David looked horrified, frightened. "What did the man do to you?"

"He told me stories, and he sounded like you, so that made me sad. When he said I was his little girl, then I thought he was going to be my new daddy, and I got . . ."

Alex stared at the photo in the locket, the photo of the man who'd not only fathered Gracie, but who'd also kidnapped her for money. But parents were supposed to protect their children not only from the evil in the world but sometimes, just sometimes, from the evil within. She looked at David and whispered, "He's her father."

"I'm her father," David said. "Don't ever say that again."

Gracie took the locket, then turned to her daddy. "Can I take this upstairs, 'cause Grandma Cecile would like to see the beautiful picture of Mommy?"

"Is Grandma Cecile okay?" David asked, obviously terrified Gracie's entire world was shattering.

"Grandma Cecile got tired from drinking tea and went to lie down in her bed. She told me to wake her up when Uncle Warren comes, but where is he?"

Alex and David stood there, neither able to speak.

Gracie put her hands on her hips and waited impatiently, looking from one to the other.

David pulled Gracie to his lap and started to tell her a story, a story about Uncle Warren, a story about how he went to visit her mommy in heaven, a story that made her cry.

"Daddy, you told me only Mommy was going to die and no one else." Gracie sobbed into her Chicken Love's belly and went upstairs to her grandma Cecile.

As soon as Gracie left the family room, David wiped a tear from his cheek and turned to Alex. "How did she get that locket?"

Alex looked at him, knowing what she was about to say would hurt him to his core. "I found it in one of Harper's shoe boxes, and I . . ."

"Why didn't you tell me?"

"I couldn't hurt you."

◆ ◆ ◆

Suddenly, they heard a motorcycle outside.

Gracie and the boys ran downstairs.

Obviously frightened and clutching her Chicken Love to her, Gracie rushed to her father. "Daddy, they're after me again."

David picked her up and hugged her. "Gracie girl, it's a surprise, and it's a good surprise."

Suddenly, there were the sounds of more motorcycles, lot of cycles, right outside their front door. David carried Gracie outside.

Eight grizzly male and two female bikers were thundering up the driveway.

Gracie stood transfixed as ten motorcycles came to a screeching halt. The motorcyclists all got off their bikes, parked them along the driveway, and lined up along the walkway, five bikers on one side facing five bikers on the other side, each one clad in a black leather vest with the logo BACA, Bikers Against Child Abuse, and their names embroidered in red letters. Bikers of various ages from about thirty to sixty, all in jeans and black biker boots, stood and waited.

As soon as David put Gracie down, she refused to move from the doorway and hugged his leg.

"They won't hurt you," David said, and lifted her up again.

"Daddy, uh, I think they got lost."

"What are they doing here?" Eric walked to the driveway.

"Daddy, they belong at the raceway like in the movie *Cars*. You saw it with me." Gracie held on to David.

He whispered something to her and pointed to the bikers.

The first biker in line, Biker Dad, red bandana around his forehead and long gray hair pulled back in a ponytail, held up a teddy bear. The bear, just like one any kid would keep on his bed, had a bright yellow shirt and white vest just like Winnie the Pooh. Biker Dad looked at the bear. It wasn't an ordinary look; it was a deep, loving look.

"That bear looks like the one you gave me long, long ago when I was little," Jon said to Alex.

Alex laughed. Jon's references to times when he was little always amused her, now that he thought he was big, grown up. She smiled and said, "Watch what they're going to do with the bear."

Biker Dad, clad in a red plaid shirt covering his big belly and bursting out from his vest, looked at the bear again. Then he brought the bear to his chest and hugged it. It wasn't just a hug but a filling of the bear with love, palpable love.

"Why does that big man have a kid's stuffed animal?" Jon asked.

"Watch," Alex said.

Biker Dad turned to Scorpio, the next biker in line. Scorpio, with closely cropped brown hair, clad in a blue and white pin-striped shirt, looked like a typical businessman—that was, except for the biker vest. Scorpio and Biker Dad looked at each other. Then they nodded. Almost at the same time, they both reached out and hugged each other with the bear in between them, receiving their love. They stopped, looked directly into each other's eyes, and smiled. Then they nodded at each other again.

Scorpio took the bear, held it against his heart, and turned to Biker Morticia. They, too, smiled at each other and nodded, knowing the bear was receiving their love. Biker Morticia put out her arms, hugged Scorpio, and patted his back before taking the bear.

Biker Morticia, with her long blonde hair cascading down from under her black leather cap, held the bear to her chest for a while, gave it a kiss on the cheek. She adjusted the bear's little white vest. Then she turned to Santa Claus, the next biker in line.

Santa Claus, with his thick white beard and long white hair, took the bear. He and Morticia hugged. They passed the bear from biker to biker until they were certain it was filled with love, protective love, just what Gracie needed.

The bear's journey continued, until the last biker in line, Viper, hugged the bear and then handed it to Gracie. "You have to keep the bear safe. If the bear feels empty and needs to be filled up with love, you must call us. We'll come to you and fill the bear up with love."

"That was weird," Eric said. "Who are they?"

Alex said, "They're part of the Orange County chapter of BACA, the—"

"We read about them in Health," Daniel said. "I know they go to the kids who've had bad stuff happen to them, like Gracie, and then they give the kid a bear."

"Yes," Alex said. "They fill the bear up with love and then hope the children keep feeling the love whenever they hold the bear."

"I get it." Daniel looked up at her. "The guy, Viper—funny name, but whatever—said when the bear is empty, the kid's supposed to call. So, when the kid is afraid, the kid is supposed to call the bikers to help."

"They want the kid to feel safe, like they're always protected even if the bikers aren't with the child. Actually, I heard they sometimes stay with the child for hours, sometimes they even sleep by the kid's bed if the kid is in the hospital," Alex said.

That night, after David read a story to Gracie, Alex, too, went into her bedroom to kiss her good night. Gracie was clutching her yellow chicken, Chicken Love, in one hand and the bear that was filled with love in her other hand.

Alex told her a story—one where children were loved, and no one ever harmed little girls.

EPILOGUE

For many, the Super Bowl is beer, chips, pizza, big-budget ads, and friends surrounding the flat-screen, but most people don't think of the major spikes in sex trafficking that accompany Super Bowl Sunday. Texas Attorney General Greg Abbott was quoted in *USA Today*, saying, "Super Bowl Sunday is commonly known as the single largest human trafficking incident in the United States."

In 2017, U.S. police arrested approximately 750 people on Super Bowl Sunday.

On February 20, 2022, Super Bowl Sunday, Child Rescue found Tara Brunner and five other girls in a parked van, held in captivity by a known trafficker for the past five years.

ACKNOWLEDGMENTS

Thank you to my amazingly supportive, but brutally honest beta readers: Tessa Kershnar, Sandra Biskind, Sandy Ponsot, Sara Bayliss, Tina Epstein, Dr. Barbara Young, Dr. Cecile Licauco, and Lisi Harrison. Wayne Bayliss proofed the novel FIVE times, cried each time, and provided both plot and editorial pearls. Your critiques gave me the encouragement and guidance I needed to polish my novel.

On my writer's journey, the following people have gone above and beyond in order to move my novel from page to media: Les Brown Jr., for making me a better speaker than I could ever have imagined. Ruth Garcia Corales, Ruth Klein, Diana Sabatino, and Aina Hoskins for supporting and scheduling my 2019 across-the-country publicity tour. Tanya Target for alerting the media! Craig Duswalt's RockStar Mastermind, eWomen, and the International Association of Women for providing the supportive communities which gave wings to my dream.

Most importantly, I want to acknowledge Peter Donovan, the CEO of Child Rescue, for not only the work his organization does to save children, but also for his inspiration and support on this project.

CPSIA information can be obtained
at www.ICGtesting.com
Printed in the USA
LVHW081633080419
613372LV00027B/1221/P